英文

日本 絵 とき事典 4
ILLUSTRATED
FESTIVALS OF JAPAN

[日本のまつり]

ILLUSTRATED
FESTIVALS OF JAPAN

©1987 by Japan Travel Bureau, Inc.
All rights reserved.

1st edition.........Jul., 1985
3rd edition........Sep., 1987

Printed in Japan

About this Book

1) Layout

   This book is divided into four main sections entitled
   Festivals throughout Japan, Curious Festivals, Annual
   Events, and Some Useful Information. 271 festivals
   are introduced, grouped according to the month in
   which they are held. The main festivals in each locality
   are shown on the book's Festival Map of Japan, and all
   the festivals are listed in the Festival Calendar.

2) Japanese Words

   All the Japanese words in this book have been roman-
   ized in accordance with the revised Hepburn system.
   Except for place names, all Japanese words are printed
   in italics except where they appear in headings or bold
   type. Long vowels are indicated by a line above, as in
   'shintō', and, since e's at the ends of words are not
   silent in Japanese, they are marked with an acute
   accent, as in 'saké' (pronounced "sahkay").

Dear Readers

Matsuri (Japanese festivals), besides reflecting the ancient religious beliefs of the country, richly depict its people's traditional customs, lifestyle and view of nature. From the vast number of festivals, annual events, and performing arts still found in every region of Japan, we have selected 271 of the most colorful and interesting for this book. We hope the descriptions and illustrations presented here will help you gain a deeper understanding of the origins of Japan's culture and the traditional thought of its people; an understanding still highly relevant to the Japan of today.

But simply to read is not to experience. Japanese festivals are popular events in which many people can take part, as performer or spectator. We urge you to join actively in as many festivals as you can, and experience Japan's ancient culture for yourself; and if the information-packed pages of this book can help you to do this, we will be more than happy.

Contents

Festivals throughout Japan

Curious Festivals

6

Annual Events

Some Useful Information

FESTIVAL MAP OF JAPAN

This map shows the more important of the 271 festivals introduced in this book.

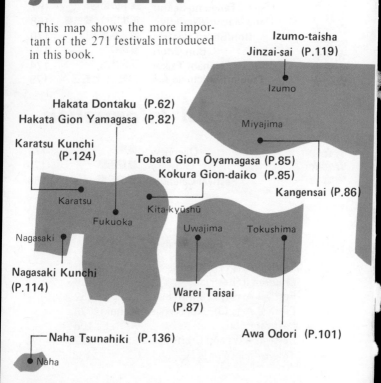

Izumo-taisha
Jinzai-sai (P.119)

Izumo

Hakata Dontaku (P.62)
Hakata Gion Yamagasa (P.82)

Miyajima

Karatsu Kunchi
(P.124)

Tobata Gion Ōyamagasa (P.85)
Kokura Gion-daiko (P.85)

Kangensai (P.86)

Karatsu

Kita-kyūshū

Fukuoka

Uwajima

Tokushima

Nagasaki

Nagasaki Kunchi
(P.114)

Warei Taisai
(P.87)

Naha Tsunahiki (P.136)

Awa Odori (P.101)

Naha

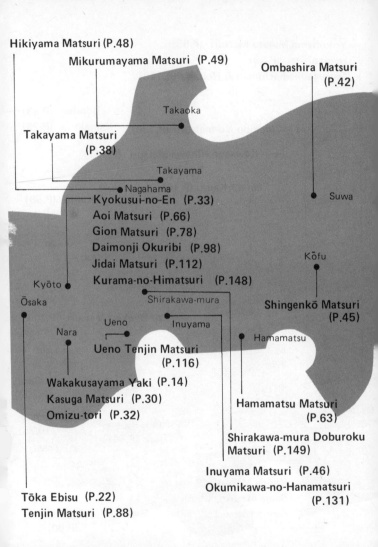

Hikiyama Matsuri (P.48)

Mikurumayama Matsuri (P.49)

Ombashira Matsuri
(P.42)

Takaoka

Takayama Matsuri
(P.38)

Takayama

Nagahama

Kyokusui-no-En (P.33)
Aoi Matsuri (P.66)
Gion Matsuri (P.78)
Daimonji Okuribi (P.98)
Jidai Matsuri (P.112)
Kurama-no-Himatsuri (P.148)

Suwa

Kōfu

Shingenkō Matsuri
(P.45)

Kyōto

Ōsaka

Shirakawa-mura

Nara

Ueno

Inuyama

Hamamatsu

Ueno Tenjin Matsuri
(P.116)

Wakakusayama Yaki (P.14)
Kasuga Matsuri (P.30)
Omizu-tori (P.32)

Hamamatsu Matsuri
(P.63)

Shirakawa-mura Doburoku
Matsuri (P.149)

Inuyama Matsuri (P.46)
Okumikawa-no-Hanamatsuri
(P.131)

Tōka Ebisu (P.22)
Tenjin Matsuri (P.88)

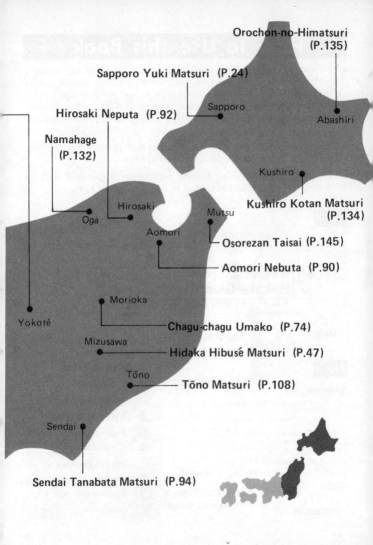

Orochon-no-Himatsuri (P.135)

Sapporo Yuki Matsuri (P.24)

Hirosaki Neputa (P.92)

Namahage (P.132)

Sapporo

Abashiri

Kushiro

Kushiro Kotan Matsuri (P.134)

Hirosaki

Oga

Mutsu

Aomori

Osorezan Taisai (P.145)

Aomori Nebuta (P.90)

Yokoté

Morioka

Chagu-chagu Umako (P.74)

Mizusawa

Hidaka Hibusé Matsuri (P.47)

Tōno

Tōno Matsuri (P.108)

Sendai

Sendai Tanabata Matsuri (P.94)

How to Use this Book

- Festivals are either introduced individually, or in groups under a particular theme. In the first case, the date of the festival and its location (shrine or temple if applicable; city, town or village; prefecture) are given under the main heading, as shown in Fig. 1; while in the second case, this information is given under the explanation of each festival, as in Fig. 2.

- Transport details and other information is given for the major festivals only. This information is enclosed in a box.

- Japanese terms requiring further explanation are marked with an asterisk in the text and explained in the Glossary (p. 179).

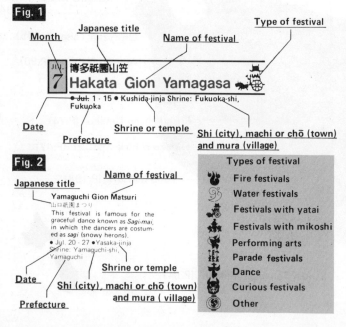

Fig. 1

Month — Japanese title — Name of festival — Type of festival

JUL.
7 博多祇園山笠
Hakata Gion Yamagasa

● Jul. 1 - 15 ● Kushida-jinja Shrine: Fukuoka-shi, Fukuoka

Date — Shrine or temple — Prefecture — Shi (city), machi or chō (town) and mura (village)

Fig. 2

Japanese title — Name of festival

Yamaguchi Gion Matsuri
山口祇園まつり
This festival is famous for the graceful dance known as *Sagi-mai*, in which the dancers are costumed as *sagi* (snowy herons).
● Jul. 20 - 27 ●Yasaka-jinja Shrine: Yamaguchi-shi, Yamaguchi

Date — Shrine or temple — Prefecture — Shi (city), machi or chō (town) and mura (village)

Types of festival	
🐦	Fire festivals
	Water festivals
	Festivals with yatai
	Festivals with mikoshi
	Performing arts
	Parade festivals
	Dance
	Curious festivals
	Other

FESTIVALS THROUGHOUT JAPAN

Japan was originally a nation of farmers, and each small farming community had its own local festivals. These festivals, depicting the people's awe of nature, their prayers for a good harvest, and their gratitude if their prayers were answered, are celebrated with tremendous energy and vitality even today. Through the illustrations and explanations in this book, you too can enter the fascinating world of Japanese festivals.

JAN. 1

若草山焼き
Wakakusayama Yaki

● Jan. 15 ● Wakakusayama: Nara-shi, Nara

Wakakusayama Yaki (The Mt. Wakakusa Fire Festival), held at night near the city of Nara, ranks with *Daimonji Okuribi* (Aug. 15; see p.98) as one of this ancient capital's most spectacular festivals. Fireworks are set off, and priests from the two temples of Tōdai-ji and Kōfuku-ji set light to the dry grass on the slopes of Mt. Wakakusa, to the east of the city; the whole mountain quickly becomes a burning beacon lighting up the night sky.

- Get off at Nara Station on the JR Line
- The fire is lit at 6 p.m.
- The best place to view the fire is from Nara Park; the buildings in the city center are too high

Wakakusayama
Mt. Wakakusa is 342 m. high and has an area of 33 ha.. It consists of three rounded hills with gentle grassy slopes and is also known as Mikasayama. (The Three Bamboo Hats).

Hanabi
Fireworks

Kōfuku-ji Temple

Kōfuku-ji Temple is located at the west end of Nara Park, about five minutes' walk from the city center. In addition to its five-storied pagoda, it also boasts the Kokuhō-kan, a museum housing more than 10,000 Buddhas, art objects and other national treasures.

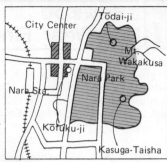

Kōfuku-ji's Pagoda

Kōfuku-ji's Five-storied Pagoda, 50.8 m. high, is the second highest pagoda in Japan. Built in the Tempyō Era (8th century) style, it is one of Nara's most famous symbols, along with the great statue of Buddha at Tōdai-ji Temple. One of Japan's best-known images is this pagoda silhouetted in the light of the fires on Mt. Wakakusa.

正月の火まつり
New Year Fire Festivals

In various parts of Japan, New Year decorations are taken down and burnt, mainly at *Koshōgatsu*, the period from the 14th to the 16th of January. This custom, supposed to bring happiness in the coming year, is known by a variety of names, such as *Sai-no-Kami*, *Dondo Yaki*, and *Sagichō*.

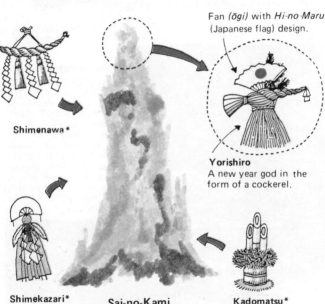

Fan *(ōgi)* with *Hi-no-Maru* (Japanese flag) design.

Shimenawa *

Yorishiro
A new year god in the form of a cockerel.

Shimekazari *

Kadomatsu *

Sai-no-Kami
賽の神
A cone-shaped bonfire of straw and bamboo is made, and the New Year decorations are burnt on it.
● Jan. 15 ● Ojiya-shi, Niigata

Nobori
Cloth streamers
on long poles

Suzumi

Morozaki-no-Sagichō
師崎の左義長

The *Sagicho* festival held at Morozaki is an exciting, lively festival at which giant *nobori* are dipped repeatedly into the flames of a bonfire onto which the New Year's decorations are thrown.

● The Sunday nearest to Jan. 2 by the lunar calendar* ● Chita-shi, Aichi

Toba-no-Himatsuri
鳥羽の火まつり

In this fire festival, two young men try to pull out sacred poles from the centers of two huge burning torches called *suzumi*. The vigor of the fire and the speed with which the young men save the sapling are omens of the coming year's fortunes.

● The Sunday nearest to Jan. 7 by the lunar calendar ● Shinmyō-ji Temple: Hazu-chō, Aichi

Mochi — Pounded rice cakes
Dango — Rice-flour dumplings

Dango and *mochi* cooked by the heat of the bonfire at the New Year Fire Festival are said to protect those who eat them from illness.

Kotefuri — leader
Gasshō — oaken staffs

Oniyo
鬼夜

This is a fire festival designed to drive away bad luck and make the new year a happy one. Huge torches called *taimatsu*, 1.5 m. in diameter, are set alight and held aloft.

● Jan. 7 ● Tamasu-jinja Shrine: Kurumé-shi, Fukuoka

裸まつり
Hadaka Matsuri

Hadaka Matsuri (literally, 'naked festivals') are a type of festival that can be seen all over Japan, at New Year and other times, in which the participants, usually young men, are naked except for loincloths. In some of these festivals, the participants jostle and fight with each other to obtain good fortune.

Yanaizu Hadaka Mairi

柳津裸参り

At 8 p.m., the temple bell is sounded, and hordes of half-naked youths and young men attempt to clamber up a thick rope suspended from the ceiling of the temple building. The first to the top will have the best fortune in the coming year.

● Jan. 7 ● Enzō-ji Temple: Yanaizu-chō, Fukushima

Onizawa Banchō Mairi

鬼沢元朝参り

Young men wearing only *mawashi* approach the shrine and make offerings of *shimenawa**.

● Jan. 1 by the lunar calendar*
● Oni-jinja Shrine: Hirosaki-shi, Aomori

Fundoshi or Mawashi

A traditional loincloth consisting of a long white cloth wound about the waist.

Kompira Hadaka Mairi

金比羅裸参り

After a purification rite in which they immerse themselves semi-naked in a nearby river, the participants in this ceremony offer candles and other gifts to the shrine.

● Jan. 10 by the lunar calendar
● Kompira-jinja Shrine: Nishiki-mura, Akita

Koshi-mino

An underskirt made of straw.

Komé-dawara
Rice bale

Shimba
Sacred horse

Tokimata-no-Hadaka Matsuri

時又の裸まつり

The semi-naked participants, bearing *mikoshi** in the form of horses, rice bales or *saké* barrels, jump into a river.

● The nearest Sunday to *hatsu-uma** (the first Horse Day in Feb.) by the lunar calendar ● Chōkoku-ji Temple: Iida-shi, Nagano

Festival Arts 1
まつりの芸能

Kagura/神楽

Kagura is the name of the sacred music and dance performed at *Shintō** festivals. The performances vary from region to region but usually consist of mythical and legendary tales mimed by masked actors accompanied by a *kagura-bayashi*, or *kagura* orchestra of flutes *(fué)*, drums *(taiko)* and other instruments.

Kazami-no-Kagura
風見の神楽

This is a *kagura* performance of one of Japan's best-known legends, *Iwato-Biraki**

● Apr. 3 ● Tōgo-jinja Shrine: Shioya-chō, Tochigi

Kamado

Tōyama-no-Shimotsuki Matsuri
遠山の霜月まつり

This festival is an example of *yutaté kagura,* a *kagura* performance featuring a *kamado,* or furnace, on which water is boiled.

● Dec. 3 - 16 ● Minamishinano-mura, Kami-mura, Nagano

Sanzoro Matsuri
参候まつり

At this festival, a unique form of *kagura* featuring *shichifukujin** is performed.

● The nearest Saturday to Nov. 17 ● Tsushima-jinja Shrine: Shitara-chō, Aichi

Nihontō

Honkawa Kagura

本川神楽

A *kagura* version of the sword dance, performed with Japanese swords *(nihontō)*.

● From the middle of Nov. to the first part of Dec. ● Honkawanai-jinja Shrine: Honkawa-mura, Kōchi

Myōga Kagura

名荷神楽

A form of *kagura* famous for its straw doll which utters divine revelations.

● Apr. 3 ● ikushi-jinja Shrine: Setoda-chō, Hiroshima

Takuno-no-Kodomo Kagura

宅野の子供神楽

This *kagura* play is performed by school-age children and depicts a battle between a god and a giant snake.

● Jan. 1 - 3 ● Takuno-chō, Shimané

Ino Kagura

井野神楽

Interesting for the gorgeous masks and costumes of the actors and their valiant posturing.

● Sep. 15 ● Hachimangū Shrine: Misumi-chō, Shimané

十日戎
Tōka Ebisu

● Jan. 9 - 11 ● Imamiya Ebisu-jinja Shrine: Ōsaka-shi, Ōsaka

This festival is held to pray for prosperity in business. It takes place in three parts; *Yoi Ebisu* on the 9th, *Hon Ebisu* on the 10th, and *Nokorifuku* on the 11th; and is attended by about a million people.

A feature of *Tōka Ebisu* is *Hoekago Gyōretsu*, a parade of *kago* (palanquins) bearing *geisha*.

With loud shouts of *"Shōbai hanjō de sasa motte koi!"* ("Bring us the *sasa* leaves that give prosperity!"), those attending the festival receive *fukusasa*, a lucky decoration made of *sasa* (bamboo grass) leaves.

An *omamori* (lucky charm) depicting the god Ebisu.
Ebisu — One of the *Shichifukujin** (the seven gods of good fortune), *Ebisu* is said to preside over trade and business.

ぼんでん
Bonden

● Feb. 17 ● Asahiokayama-jinja Shrine: Yokoté-shi, Akita

In the *Bonden* festival, special shrine decorations called *bonden*, each carried by 20 to 30 young men, are taken to a shrine for consecration. The rival groups shake and spin the *bonden* violently as they carry them, and compete energetically to be first to set them in place.

Bonden, one of the many kinds of religious artifact offered to the gods at *Shintō** shrines, consist of 3 m. poles wound with cloths of 5 different colors, with various ingenious decorations fixed on top.

Kawawatari Bonden

川渡りぼんでん

In this version of the *Bonden* festival, the *bonden* are ferried across a river to a shrine on the far bank.
● Feb. 17 ● Izuyama-jinja Shrine: Ōmagari-shi, Akita

札幌雪まつり
Sapporo Yukimatsuri

● Feb.5 - 11● Sapporo-shi, Hokkaidō

This festival, started in 1950, features a display of snow sculptures of all sizes from small to giant, on a different theme each year. For sheer scale and the number of visitors it attracts, this spectacle easily outranks any other of Japan's many snow festivals.

- Sapporo is the largest city in Hokkaidō, the farthest north of Japan's four main islands. It is about 1 **hr.** and 30 min. from Tōkyō by plane.
- The festival is held in Ōdōri Park (Ōdōri Kōen), which can be reached on foot from Ōdōri Station on the Tōzai or Nanboku subway lines.
- Since Sapporo is always crowded during the Snow Festival, accommodation should be reserved well in advance.

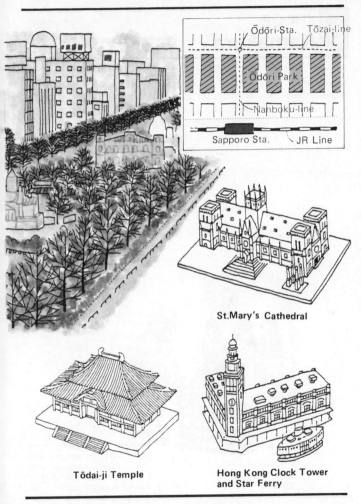

Ōdōri-Sta.　Tōzai-line

Ōdōri Park

Nanboku-line

Sapporo Sta.　　JR Line

St.Mary's Cathedral

Tōdai-ji Temple

Hong Kong Clock Tower
and Star Ferry

かまくら
Kamakura

● Feb. 15 - 17 ● Yokoté Park: Yokoté-shi, Akita

A *kamakura* is a kind of igloo made by building a mound of snow about 2 m. in diameter and hollowing out the inside. A small altar is set up inside and dedicated to *Suijin-sama*, the god of water. Children use the *kamakura* as a play house, cooking and eating *mochi** and drinking *amazaké*. Building *kamakura* is a common custom in the snowy parts of Japan.

It is surprisingly warm inside a *kamakura* — so warm that there is no need for coat, scarf, or gloves.

Mino
A kind of woven straw cape, used to protect the wearer from cold, rain and snow. Its outside has a downy appearance.

Sori
Sledge

Kamidana
A small altar — in this case, dedicated to the god of water.

Omiki
An offering of *saké* *.

Amazaké
A sweet, slightly-alcoholic drink made from fermented rice.

Hibachi
The *hibachi*, or charcoal brazier, is Japan's traditional method of heating dwellings. It can also be used to cook *mochi* or other foods.

On the day of the festival, shops sell lucky cranes and turtles made of rice flour as well as *inukko* (dog dolls).

Inukko
dog dolls

Inukko Matsuri
犬っこまつり

In this festival to the god of dogs, our protectors against robbery and other misfortunes, shrines are built of snow, and offerings of candles and *inukko* (dog dolls made of rice flour) are placed on them as a prayer for a year's good luck. *Inukko Matsuri* ranks with *Kamakura* as one of Akita's best-known winter festivals.
● Feb. 15 - 16 ● Yuzawa-shi, Akita

冬のまつり
Winter Festivals

Komedawara-hiki
米俵引き

Semi-naked young men wrestle for a large rice bale in this New Year festival. The price of rice for the year is foretold from the outcome of the contest.

● Jan. 14 ● Aizubange-machi Fukushima

Awa

The *awa* is supposed to represent a false sun, and it is stabbed with bamboo poles to exterminate all such impostors.

Gētā Matsuri
ゲーターまつり

Early on New Year's morning, young men thrust bamboo poles into a large white wheel called *awa*, and parade it aloft. The wheel is 2 m. in diameter and is made from the branches of the *gumi* (oleaster) tree.

● Jan. 1 ● Yashiro-jinja Shrine: Toba-shi, Mié

Mayu-dama

A decoration displayed at New Year to welcome the gods.

Aenokoto

アエノコト

In this festival, people invite the gods of the rice fields into their homes and treat them to a feast, in the hope of being favored with a good harvest. In the local dialect, *aé* means 'to invite someone to a meal', and *koto* means 'a family celebration'.

● Dec. 5 ● Okunoto, Ishikawa

Okonai

おこない

This special festival is held at the northern end of Lake Biwa to welcome spring. Cocoon-shaped *mochi** are hung on *kashi* (oak) branches to make the festive decoration called *mayu-dama*.

● Feb. - Mar. ● Ika-gun, Shiga

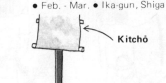

Kitchō

Bannai-san — The keeper of the *kitchō*, wearing a devil mask and the garments used in *kagura**.

Kitchō-to-Bannai-san

吉兆と番内さん

Marchers called *Bannai-san* parade the streets bearing a large *nobori** called *kitchō*.

● Jan. 3 ● Izumo-taisha Shrine: Taisha-machi, Shimané

春日まつり
Kasuga Matsuri

● Mar. 13 ● Kasuga-taisha Shrine: Nara-shi, Nara

Kasuga Matsuri is the spring festival or Nara's Kasuga-taisha Shrine. The interesting *hiki-uma* horse ceremony and the elegant *Yamato-mai* dance performed at this festival remind us of the culture and customs of the Nara and Heian Era* (8th – 12th century).

Kasuga-taisha Shrine
The construction of this famous shrine lasted from the Nara Era (8th century) into the early part of the Heian Era (9th century). It has four main buildings which enshrine four different gods, and is known for its unique style of architecture, dubbed 'Kasuga style'.

- The bus from Kintetsu Nara Station takes about 15 minutes. Get off at the Kasuga-taisha Maé stop.
- The usual route into the shrine is through the main gate, the *Ichi no Torii**.

Sacred horse

Hiki-uma
In this ceremony, a sacred horse is led in procession into the shrine precincts.

Yamato-mai
This graceful dance, unique to Japan, has been preserved over the centuries at Kasuga-taisha Shrine.

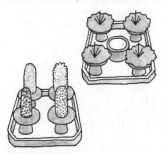

Shinsen
These religious offerings of food and drink, include items such as rice, *saké**, *mochi**, fish, chicken, and fruit. The offerings made at Kasuga-taisha are famous for their beautiful colors and artistic arrangement.

31

3 お水取り
Omizu-tori

● Mar. 1 - 14 ● Tōdai-ji Temple: Nara-shi, Nara

The *Omizu-tori* festival is part of the Tōdai-ji Temple monks' training program known as *shunié*. On the evening of Mar. 12, the monks light large *taimatsu** and wave them around from the gallery of the Nigatsudō, one of the temple buildings, showering the spectators with sparks. After this, a ceremony is performed in which water is drawn from a well.

Tōdai-ji Nigatsudō
This 8th century building features a high outer gallery from which the whole of downtown Nara can be seen.

Omizu-okuri
お水送り
In this ceremony, which takes place before *Omizu-tori*, holy water is presented to the gods.
● Mar. 2 ● Jingū-ji Temple: Obama-shi, Fukui

Dattan-no-mai
This is the name given to the dancing and waving of the torches by the monks.

● Apr. 29 ● Jōnangū Shrine: Kyōto-shi, Kyōto

Kyokusui was a pastime practiced by the nobility in ancient times in which a lacquer *saké* cup was set adrift in a stream, and the participants, sitting on a downstream bank, had to compose a short poem such as a *tanka* and then drink the *saké* when it reached them. *Kyokusui-no-En* is a re-enactment of this pastime.

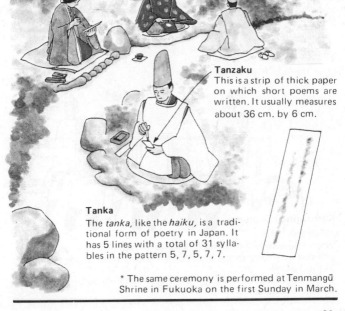

Tanzaku
This is a strip of thick paper on which short poems are written. It usually measures about 36 cm. by 6 cm.

Tanka
The *tanka,* like the *haiku,* is a traditional form of poetry in Japan. It has 5 lines with a total of 31 syllables in the pattern 5, 7, 5, 7, 7.

* The same ceremony is performed at Tenmangū Shrine in Fukuoka on the first Sunday in March.

田植えまつり
Rice-Planting Festivals

Festivals held to pray for a good harvest can be seen in all parts of Japan. Most of them either take place at the beginning of the year, when the year's farming activities are acted out in prayer for a good year, or at *taué* or rice-planting time (May – June) in prayer for a good rice crop.

Hanakazari Minogasa — Straw hat decorated with flowers.

Kamimino — Raincoat made of paper for festivals

Fujimori-no-Taasobi

藤森の田遊び

This festival features 27 different dances and is said to have a history of over 1,000 years.

● Mar. 17 ● Ōihachimangū Shrine: Ōigawa-chō, Shizuoka

Two teams of five face off and start a drinking boul.

Katori-jingū Otauesai

香取神宮御田植祭

Women known as *taué-onna* ("rice-planting women") perform the rice-planting ceremony to the music of a *hayashi** band on the second day of this festival.

● The first Saturday and Sunday in Apr. ● Katori-jingū Shrine Sawara-shi, Chiba

Otaué Shinji
御田植え神事

This festival is famous for its dance, a combination of a puppet play and *nō**.
● Apr. 13 ● Kumata-jinja Shrine: Ōsaka-shi Ōsaka

Izōnomiya Otaué Matsuri
伊雑宮御田植えまつり

This festival features boys aged 5 to 6 dressed as women and playing the *taiko* (large drum).
● Jun. 24 ● Izōnomiya Shrine: Isobé-chō, Mié

Otaué Matsuri
御田植えまつり

At this festival, a special dance known as *otaué-odori* ('the rice-planting dance') is performed.
● The nearest Sunday to Feb. 21 ● Kagami-tsukuri-jinja Shrine: Tawaramoto-chō, Nara

Onda Matsuri
おんだまつり

This festival is held after the rice planting is over, and features a parade of *unari* (women bearing a midday meal to the gods) dressed in white robes.
● Jul. 28 ● Aso-jinja Shrine: Ichinomiya-chō, Kumamoto

Mibu-no-Hana Taué
壬生の花田植え

This ceremony is known for its special *taué-uta* (rice-planting songs).
● The first Sunday in Jun. ● Chiyoda-chō, Hiroshima

Utsu-ué Matsuri
打植えまつり

This dance is performed by men wearing ox masks.
● Mar. 6 ● Yatsufusa-jinja Shrine: Kushikino-shi, Kagoshima

Children in Festivals

稚児

Young boys and girls can often be seen taking part in Buddhist and *Shintō** festivals in all areas of Japan. These child performers are known as *chigo*, and their beautiful costumes and the innocence and earnestness with which they perform the music or dance are an entrancing sight.

Hikawa-jinja Hanashizumé-no-Mai

氷川神社花鎮の舞

A ''cherry-blossom'' dance in which the children wear cherry blossoms in their hair and hold branches of blossoms.
● Apr. 5 - 7 ● Hikawa-jinja Shrine : Ōmiya-shi, Saitama

Hanaoké — Wooden tubs holding magical flowers to ward off evil

Hanaoké Katsugi

花桶かつぎ

Young girls carrying *hanaoké* walk in procession to the shrine.
● Jan. 25 ● Sankawa-temmangū Shrine: Oyama-shi, Tochigi

Akadomari Matsuri
赤泊まつり

A simple dance full of local color.
● Apr. 18 ● Wakamiya Hachiman-jinja Shrine: Akadomari-mura, Niigata

Tama-no-Kagura
田間の神楽

This *kagura** is performed by a group of 10 young girls.
● Apr. 15 - 16 ● Chigata-jinja Shrine: Oyama-shi, Tochigi

Chakkirako
チャッキラコ

An ancient dance performed by young girls dressed in *haregi* (best *kimono*). The name represents the sound of the *ayadaké,* a paper-wrapped bamboo percussion instrument, that the dancers carry.
● Jan. 15 ● Gohongū Kainan-jinja Shrine :Miura-shi, Kanagawa

Magomi Matsuri
孫見まつり

This shrine festival is held to keep the fires of Mt. Fuji quiet and prevent it erupting.
● Apr. 25 ● Kawaguchi Sengen-jinja Shrine: Kawaguchiko-machi, Yamanashi

37

高山まつり
Takayama Matsuri

● Apr. 14 - 15 ● Hie-jinja Shrine: Takayama-shi, Gifu
● Oct. 9 - 10 ● Sakuragaoka-hachimangū Shrine

This festival is held twice a year in spring and autumn, and is famous for its lavishly-decorated *yatai**, or parade floats. 12 of these appear at the spring festival and 11 at the autumn festival, and all represent the pinnacle of Japan's folk arts. The unique folk music known as *tōkeigaku* performed at the festival also leaves a lasting impression.

The parade floats at *Takayama Matsuri* are so gorgeously-decorated, with lacquered wood, embossed and engraved metal, and richly-patterned cloth, that they are referred to as "Yōmeimon in motion", Yōmeimon is the famous gate at the Tōshōgū Shrine in Nikkō.

Some of the parade floats are equipped with ingeniously-designed clockwork marionettes to entertain the crowds. These puppets are beautifully-costumed.

Tōkeigaku is a parade of gongs. The booming and ringing of the gongs helps heighten the festive atmosphere.

Shō — metal gong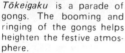

The *shishi-mai** (see p.52) of *Takayama Matsuri*.

- Take the JR Takayama Honsen Line to Takayama Station.
- Spring festival
  Apr. 14: Parade starts at 3 p.m.
  Evening events from 7 p.m. – 9 p.m. (the eve of the festival)
  Apr. 15: 9:30 a.m. – 4 p.m. (The main festival day)
- Autumn festival
  Oct. 9: Parade starts at 1 p.m.
  Evening events from 7 p.m. – 9.30 p.m. (The eve of the festival)
  Oct. 10: 8:30 a.m. – 5 p.m.

The *Hōmeidai* — this float has *shishi* (Chinese lions) carved in the *ittōbori* style above the wheels, and also features beautifully-engraved metal fittings.

The *Kyūhōsha* — one of *Takayama Matsuri's* parade floats. This is one of Japan's oldest *yatai**, and is famous for its *nishiki-é* (colored silk prints), which were imported from China in the 15th century.

Ittōbori — a style of carving requiring tremendous skill, in which a single tool is used for the whole carving.

Hotei, a Chinese Zen priest known for his unique pot-bellied appearance and deified as a Buddhist spirit of happiness and good fortune.

The puppets displayed on the *Hoteidai* float are famous for the intricacy of their actions. Two *karako* (Chinese children) swing down on a trapeze and land on the shoulders of the priest Hotei Oshō.

The *mikoshi** at the autumn festival. The *yatai* follow after.

Yatai consist of three tiers, an upper, middle and lower, and are built so that they shake and sway as they are pulled along. The carvings and silk hangings on the lower tier and the puppets on the upper tier are their most interesting features.

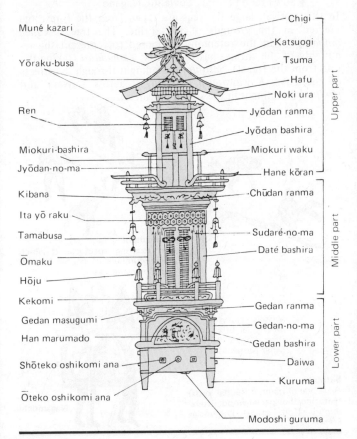

Muné kazari

Yōraku-busa

Ren

Miokuri-bashira

Jyōdan-no-ma

Kibana

Ita yō raku

Tamabusa

Ōmaku

Hōju

Kekomi

Gedan masugumi

Han marumado

Shōteko oshikomi ana

Ōteko oshikomi ana

Chigi

Katsuogi

Tsuma

Hafu

Noki ura

Jyōdan ranma

Jyōdan bashira

Miokuri waku

Hane kōran

Chūdan ranma

Sudaré-no-ma

Daté bashira

Gedan ranma

Gedan-no-ma

Gedan bashira

Daiwa

Kuruma

Modoshi guruma

Upper part

Middle part

Lower part

御柱まつり
Ombashira Matsuri

● Suwa-taisha Shrine: Suwa-shi, Nagano

In this festival, large fir trees are taken from the forest and erected in the grounds of the shrine. The tree is called *ombashira,* and the ceremony, supposed to represent the rebuilding of the shrine, has four parts; *Yamadashi* (taking the tree from the forest), *Satobiki* (parading it through the streets of the city), *Kawawatashi* (carrying it across a river), and *Hikitaté* (erecting it in the shrine precincts).

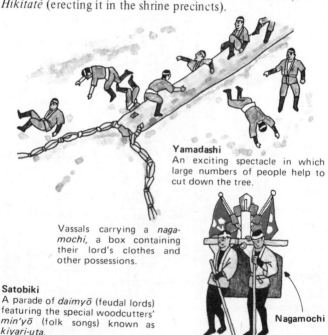

Yamadashi
An exciting spectacle in which large numbers of people help to cut down the tree.

Vassals carrying a *naga-mochi,* a box containing their lord's clothes and other possessions.

Satobiki
A parade of *daimyō* (feudal lords) featuring the special woodcutters' *min'yō* (folk songs) known as *kiyari-uta.*

Nagamochi

Ropes are tied to the top of the tree and many people help to raise it.

Hikitaté
The grand finale of the festival, when the tree is erected at one of the corners of the four shrine buildings.

• This festival is held once every 6 years, in the Year of the Monkey* and the Year of the Tiger*, from the first part of April to the middle part of May.

APR. 4 上杉まつり Uesugi Matsuri

- Apr. 29 – May 3 • Uesugi-jinja Shrine: Yonezawa-shi, Yamagata

The Sengoku (Warring States) Era* in the 15th and 16th centuries was full of heroic leaders struggling to gain supremacy over the whole of Japan, and one of the most famous of these warrior lords was Uesugi Kenshin*. This festival commemorates him and his followers with a *Musha Gyōretsu* (parade of warriors) in the costume of the times, mock battles, and other events.

Uesugi Kenshin (1530 – 1578)

The Battles of Kawanakajima

In this famous series of battles, the scene of which was a triangular island in the middle of a river, Uesugi Kenshin fought his arch-enemy Takeda Shingen*. The battles took place 5 times over a period of 12 years, but the two rivals died natural deaths before either had achieved a decisive victory.

信玄公まつり
Shingenkō Matsuri

- The Saturday and Sunday nearest to Apr. 12
- Kōfu-shi, Yamanashi

Takeda Shingen was another of the Sengoku Era's famous warriors. A well-known event at this festival, held on the anniversary of his death, is *Shutsujinshiki*, a ceremony held before a battle. After this ceremony, more than a 1,000 men dressed as soldiers stage a mock battle in the streets of the city.

Hatasashimono

These standards were carried in battle to distinguish the opposing armies. They usually carried the ruler's family crest at the top, with the names of the army's deified heroues below. Takeda Shingen's banner was famous for its motto, *Fū-rin-ka-zan* ("wind, forest, fire and mountains").

Fū (Kazé) (as swift as the wind)

Rin (Hayashi) (as silent as the forest)

Ka (Hi) (as deadly as fire)

Zan (Yama) (as unshakeable as the mountains)

Led by Takeda Shingen, 24 commanders ceremonially take the field for battle.

犬山まつり
Inuyama Matsuri

- The first or second Sunday in Apr.
- Harizuna-jinja Shrine: Inuyama-shi, Aichi

Inuyama Matsuri is the only one of Aichi's festivals to feature parade floats. There are 13 of these floats in the festival, all lavishly-decorated and dating from the Edo Era*. At night, decorated with over 300 *chōchin* (paper lanterns), they are a beautiful and unforgettable sight.

Urashima float

Shakukyō float

Yūgyoshin float

Ueyama
(The upper part of the float)
— puppet stage

Nakayama
(The middle part of the float)
— puppeteers' section

Shitayama
(The lower part of the float)
— *hayashi** (festival music) band pit

日高火防まつり
Hidaka Hibusé Matsuri

● Apr. 22 ● Hidaka-jinja Shrine: Mizusawa-shi, Iwaté

This festival originated as a rite to ward off outbreaks of fire. Musical floats parade through the town, some carrying young girls sitting on a stepped dais and beating small drums *(hayashi-yatai)*, and others with flute and drum bands.

The young girls on the *hayashi-yatai* floats, known as *saotomé**, are gaily-costumed and have many decorations in their hair.

Hibusé Matsuri
火防まつり

This festival is famous for its *Hibusé-no-Tora Mai*, similar to *shishi-mai**(The lion dance). It is also held to try to prevent fires.
● Apr. 29 ● Ōsaki-jinja Shrine: Nakaniida-machi, Miyagi

Kami-shimo — a wide-shouldered *kimono* like *hakama,* normally worn by men.

曳山まつり
Hikiyama Matsuri

● Apr. 13 - 16 ● Nagahama-hachimangū Shrine:
Nagahama-shi, Shiga

This festival features festival floats known as *Hikiyama*. The second tier at the front of these floats forms a stage on which local children aged from 5 to 12 perform *kyōgen**, *kabuki**, etc.

The child performers wear the same costumes as adults do when performing these plays.

The ornate decoration of the *Hikiyama* float provides a gorgeous backdrop for the children's performances.

御車山まつり
Mikurumayama Matsuri

● May 1 ● Kanno-jinja Shrine: Takaoka-shi, Toyama

Special festival floats known as *Mikurumayama* make their appearance at this festival. These floats are known for their beautifully-embellished wheels and the traditional craftwork displayed in their decoration.

Amusing mechanical puppets add to the enjoyment of the festivals. Many of these show a distinct Chinese influence.

Hokodomé
This represents the sun and its rays.

A wheel of the Mikurumayama Matsuri's floats

The intricate metalwork on the large, black-lacquered wheels of the float is almost dazzlingly bright.

Shōgawa-chō-no-Yotaka Matsuri

庄川町の夜高まつり

The brightly-lit floats known as *andon-dashi* which appear at this festival in the evening make a beautiful sight.
● May 10 ● Shōgawa-chō, Toyama

Andon
—An ancient type of night lamp stand.

Mikuni Matsuri

三国まつり

This is one of the three biggest festivals in the Hokuriku region, and is known for its 5 m. high festival floats with their huge carvings of *musha* (warriors).
● May 19 - 21 ● Mikuni-jinja Shrine: Mikuni-shi, Fukui

Seihakusai

青柏祭

The floats used at this festival are called *dekayama* (huge mountains) because of their giant size. Each one is about 13 m. high, has wheels 2 m. in diameter, and weighs 20 tons. They are equipped with stages on which mechanical dolls perform well-known *kabuki*＊ scenes.
● May 13 - 15 ● Ōtokonushi-jinja Shrine: Nanao-shi, Ishikawa

Kodomo-kabuki Hikiyama Matsuri

子供歌舞伎曳山まつり

Children give enthusiastic performances of *kabuki* on the stages built on the festival floats used at this festival.

● Apr. 16 - 17 ● Demachi-shin-myōsha Shrine: Tonami-shi, Toyama

Kutami-no-Itokiri Karakuri

久田見の糸切りからくり

This festival features puppets operated by a cogwheel-and-thread mechanism known as *Itokiri Karakuri*.

● Apr. 4 - 5 ● Shirahigé-jinja Shrine: Yaotsu-chō, Gifu

Tarui Hikiyama Matsuri

垂井曳山まつり

At this festival, children perform *kabuki* on the stages of lavishly-decorated three-storied festival floats.

● May 2 - 4 ● Yaegaki-jinja Shrine : Tarui-chō, Gifu

Festival Arts 2

まつりの芸能

Shishi-mai/獅子舞い

Shishi-mai (the Lion Dance) features the *shishi*, or Chinese lion. The dance was originally used by Japanese farmers as a spell to ward off, not lions, since these are not indigenous to Japan, but wild boar and other animals which cause damage to crops. Each region has its own unique variation of the dance.

Nagaori-no-Sanbiki Jishi
長折の三匹獅子

Performed on a colorfully-decorated stage.
● Apr. 27 ● Suma-jinja Shrine: Iwashiro-machi, Fukushima

Koina-no-Tora-mai
小稲の虎舞い

This dance is performed on a stage called *tora-yama* built on the beach.
● Aug. 14 by the lunar calendar*
● Raigū-jinja Shrine: Minamiizu-chō, Shizuoka

Nagi Hachiman-jinja Aki Matsuri
梛八幡神社秋まつり

Well-known for its 12 different types of *shishimai*
● Oct. 20 ● Nagi-hachiman-jinja Shrine: Tatsuno-shi, Hyōgo

Tanahashi Okashira Shinji

棚橋御頭神事

Okashira refers to the head of the lion. This festival features 2 types of dance; *Zashiki-mai,* which takes place in the daytime, and *Uchi-matsuri,* in the evening.
● Jan. 12 by the lunar calendar *
● Watarai-chō, Mié

Kamuro-jinja Aki Matsuri

冠纓神社秋まつり

The head of the lion used in the *shishi-mai* at this festival is 165 cm. tall and 180 cm. wide.
● Oct. 18 ● Kamuro-jinja Shrine: Kōnan-chō, Kagawa

Kurata-hachimangū-Sai

倉田八幡宮祭

A special type of lion dance called *Kirin* Jishi-mai,* featuring the mythical beast *kirin.*
● Apr. 15 ● Kurata-hachimangū Shrine: Tottori-shi, Tottori

Shirotori-jinja Aki Matsuri

白鳥神社秋まつり

Instead of a lion, the main attraction at this festival is a huge tiger dancing ferociously.
● Oct. 6 - 8 ● Shirotori-jinja Shrine: Shirotori-chō, Kagawa

東京のまつり
Festivals in Tōkyō

In Tōkyō the use of festival floats was stopped at the end of the Meiji Era in the last century, since the roofs of these floats were fouling the overhead power lines. Instead, the *mikoshi** in each locality are brought out on festival days, paraded around the area with lusty shouts by men and women wearing *hachimaki* (headbands) and *matsuri-hanten* (special short coats for festivals), and carried to a local shrine for the grand finale. Recently, *mikoshi* carried by teams composed entirely of women have made an appearance. These are called *Onna-mikoshi*.

Kanda Ichiba *(yachaba)*'s *mikoshi* being taken out of the shrine.

Kanda Matsuri

神田まつり

This is one of the three biggest festivals of Edo* (the old name of Tōkyō). 70 *mikoshi* take part, the biggest being the *Sengan-Mikoshi* of Kanda Ichiba.

● May 12 - 16 ● Kanda-jinja Shrine: Chiyoda-ku, Tōkyō

Gold *shishi-gashira* (lions' heads) are paraded as well as the *mikoshi*.

A parade of *hōren* (wheeled *mikoshi)* pulled by oxen.

Geisha performing the *Teko-mai* dance add color to the proceedings.

Kappa Tennōsai

かっぱ天王祭

In prayer for a good harvest and rich hauls of fish, the local people carry *mikoshi* into the sea.
- The Saturday and Sunday nearest to Jun. 7
- Ebara-jinja Shrine: Shinagawa-ku, Tōkyō

Sanja Matsuri

三社まつり

Probably the most famous of Tōkyō's festivals, the *Sanja Matsuri* attracts a great number of spectators. On the Saturday, more than 100 *machi-mikoshi*, large and small, are paraded through the streets; and on the Sunday, the main festival day, the three main *honja-mikoshi* make their ceremonial exit from Asakusa-jinja Shrine, the shrine where they are housed.

● The three days centered around the third Sunday in May
● Asakusa-jinja Shrine: Taitō-ku, Tōkyō

There are three *honja-mikoshi* — *Ichi-no-Miya*, *Ni-no-Miya* and *San-no-Miya*.

Binzasara

In the dance known as *binzasara-mai*, the dancers beat time with *binzasara*, percussion instruments made from wooden slats tied with cord.

Torigoé Matsuri

鳥越まつり

Lit by many *chōchin**, the *mikoshi* at this festival are a beautiful sight as they return to the shrine in the evening.

● The nearest Sunday to Jun. 9
● Torigoé-jinja Shrine: Taitō-ku, Tōkyō

Sumida Inari-jinja Sairei

隅田稲荷神社祭礼

An illuminated *mikoshi* called *Mantō-mikoshi* ("*mikoshi* of 10,000 lanterns") appears at this festival.

● The nearest Saturday and Sunday to Jun. 15 ● Sumida Inari-jinja Shrine: Sumida-ku, Tōkyō

Tsukuda Matsuri

佃まつり

This festival features an unusual eight-sided 19th-century *mikoshi*.
● The three days centered on Aug. 6 ● Sumiyoshi-jinja Shrine: Chūō-ku, Tōkyō

Grabbing the lion's nose at the *Tsukuda Matsuri* is said to bring good luck.

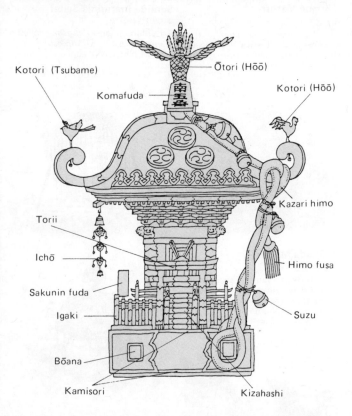

Kotori (Tsubame)

Ōtori (Hōō)

Komafuda

Kotori (Hōō)

南玉苗

Kazari himo

Torii

Ichō

Himo fusa

Sakunin fuda

Igaki

Suzu

Bōana

Kamisori

Kizahashi

The word *mikoshi* is written with the characters for *kami* (god) and *kago*, or *koshi* (palanquin). Those of a religious turn of mind believe that when a *mikoshi* is taken out and paraded around, the local guardian deity descends into it for the ride. There are many types of *mikoshi*, but most are made of black-lacquered wood with a *hōō* (Chinese phoenix) or other ornamental device on the top.

I-gumi Kurenai-kai Goku Sanban-gumi

Ikku Ichiban-gumi Edoryū Asakusa Ayamé-ren

Goku Goban-gumi Miyoshi-kai Iroha-kai

A *hanten* decorated on the back with the symbol of the local *mikoshi* group is customary wear at festivals. This symbol, called *daimon*, is usually designed to incorporate the crest or other logo of the local town association. The overall dress for *mikoshi* carriers is modelled on that of a *tobi*, or Edo Era* fireman.

MAY. 5 日立風流物
Hitachi Furyūmono

● May 3 - 5 ● Hitachi-shi, Ibaraki

Festival floats featuring puppets are termed *furyūmono*. The ones displayed at this festival in Hitachi-shi are particularly large, and are up to 15 m. tall. The puppets mounted on them perform various dramas.

The front of a *furyūmono* is called *Omoté-yama* and the back *Ushiro-yama*. *Omoté-yama* has 5 tiers of puppets, with a 7-pr 8-man *narimono-gakari* (orchestra) and 25 to 26 puppeteers inside.

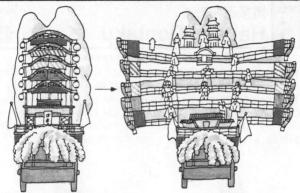

Omoté-yama (the front part of the float) with its stage doors closed. The doors open to left and right to display the puppets performing their plays.

The main plays performed by *Omoté-yama*'s puppets are simplified versions of Edo Era* works.

So as to be invisible to the spectators, the puppeteers lie on their backs while operating the puppets.

Ushiro-yama (the rear part of the float) is built like a huge rock. Its puppets perform nursery tales and fables.

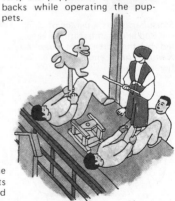

博多どんたく
Hakata Dontaku

● May 2 - 4 ● Fukuoka-shi, Fukuoka

The name *Dontaku* is a corruption of the Dutch word Zontag, meaning Sunday. The festival is said to have started as a New Year parade of merchants going to the local lord's residence to celebrate. About 30,000 of the local townspeople take part, and its attractions include the traditional *Matsubayashi* parade, a fancy-dress parade and a *shamoji* band.

Matsubayashi is a parade of children and adults in traditional dress, led by the three gods *Fuku-no-Kami, Ebisu* and *Daikoku,* on horseback.

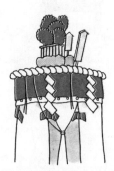

The *kasahoko,* a float that forms part of the *Matsubayashi* parade. It is believed in Fukuoka that babies carried under the *kasahoko* will grow up strong and healthy.

The *shamoji* band parades around the town beating time with *shamoji,* the wooden spatulas used for serving rice.

● May 3 - 5 ● Hamamatsu-shi, Shizuoka

Apart from the festival float parade in the town itself, the main attraction of this festival is the kite battle held on the long beach at Nakatajima, in which each local association flies its own giant kite and attempts to cut the strings of rival kites.

The kites range in size from 3 m. square to 6 m. square, and hundreds of excited people help to manipulate them in the battles.

In the evening, a richly-decorated float called *goten-yatai* is paraded through the streets.

東照宮春の大祭
Tōshōgū Haru-no-Taisai

● May 17 - 18 ● Tōshōgū Shrine: Nikkō-shi, Tochigi

This festival is held at the Tōshōgū shrine in Nikkō in honor of the first *shōgun** of the Edo Era*, Tokugawa Ieyasu*. The highlight of the festival is the parade known as *Hyakumono-zoroi Sennin Musha Gyōretsu*, featuring the traditional costumes of the era, on May 18.

**Hyakumonozoroi
Sennin Musha
Gyōretsu**

In the parade, beautifully-costumed children march together with adults dressed as *samurai* in helmets and armor. More than 1,200 people take part.

● Take the Tōbu bus from the JR Nikkō Station and get off at Shinkyō, Tōshōgū is 10 minutes' walk.
● The parade leaves Futarasan-jinja Shrine at 11 a.m. and proceeds along Omotesandō Street towards Otabisho before returning to Tōshōgū Shrine.
● The best place to watch the parade from is Omotesandō Street.

横浜港まつり
Yokohama Minato Matsuri

● May 3 - Jul. 20 ● Yokohama-shi, Kanagawa

The festival (Yokohama Port Festival) is held to commemorate the opening of the Port of Yokohama on Jun. 2, 1859. The highlight of the festival is the International Fancy Dress Parade held on May 3, in which over 3,000 people, including many non-Japanese residents, take part. The parade stretches out for as much as 2 km.

Kurofuné* Matsuri
黒船まつり

This festival is held to commemorate the arrival of America's Commodore Perry off Shimoda, a small fishing town at the south end of the Izu Peninsula. The festival has an international flavor and features a U.S. Navy parade among its many events.
● May 16 - 18 ● Shimoda-shi, Shizuoka

葵まつり
Aoi Matsuri

● May 15 ● Shimogamo-jinja and Kamigamo-jinja Shrines:
Kyōto-shi, Kyōto

This festival boasts a history of 1,400 years. Its main attraction is an elegant parade known as *Rotō-no-gi*, which features ox-drawn carriages together with 600 people dressed in the costumes of *ōmiyabito*, Heian* (9th – 12th century) court nobles. The parade starts at Kyōto Palace and proceeds via Shimogamo-jinja to Kamigamo-jinja Shrine.

The festival derives its name from the *katsura* or *aoi* leaves carried by the participants and used to adorn the oxen, horses, and carriages.

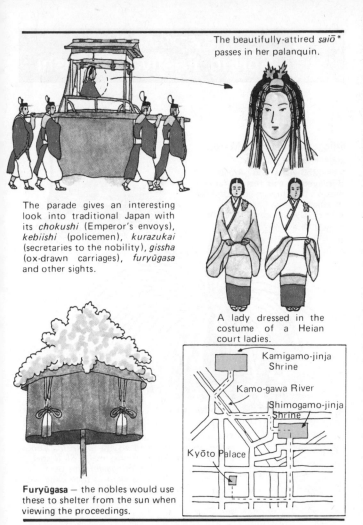

The beautifully-attired *saiō* *
passes in her palanquin.

The parade gives an interesting
look into traditional Japan with
its *chokushi* (Emperor's envoys),
kebiishi (policemen), *kurazukai*
(secretaries to the nobility), *gissha*
(ox-drawn carriages), *furyūgasa*
and other sights.

A lady dressed in the
costume of a Heian
court ladies.

Kamigamo-jinja
Shrine

Kamo-gawa River

Shimogamo-jinja
Shrine

Kyōto Palace

Furyūgasa — the nobles would use
these to shelter from the sun when
viewing the proceedings.

Shiogama-jinja Hoté Matsuri
塩竈神社帆手まつり

The 250-years old *Ara-Mikoshi* displayed at this festival ranks as one of the three biggest *mikoshi* in Japan.
● Mar. 10 ● Shiogama-jinja Shrine : Shiogama-shi, Miyagi

Shinai

Mino Matsuri
美濃まつり

This festival is notable for the floral decorations called *shinai* attached to the *mikoshi*. About 200 of these decorations, made of a special kind of paper called *minogami*, are used, and they make a beautiful sight as they sway with the motion of the *mikoshi*.
● Apr. 14 - 15 ● Hachiman-jinja Shrine: Mino-shi, Gifu

Saka-oroshi Matsuri

坂下しまつり

At this festival, the *mikoshi* are lowered with straw ropes down a steep hill 600 m. long with a vertical drop of 150 m.
- The first Sunday in May
- Ōhama, Bōko, Kinuminé-jinja Shrine: Notogawa-chō, Shiga

Sagichō Matsuri

左義長まつり

Young men dressed as women carry *mikoshi*-style floats decorated with the animal of the year accoding to the Chinese calendar*.
- A Saturday and Sunday in the middle of Mar.
- Himuré-hachiman-jinja Shrine: Ōmi-hachiman-shi, Shiga

Ichinomiya Kenka Matsuri

一の宮けんかまつり

At this festival, two *mikoshi* teams shove and fight to be first to have their *mikoshi* consecrated at the shrine.
- Apr. 10 ● Amatsu-jinja Shrine: Itoigawa-shi, Niigata

69

春のまつり
Spring Festivals

Furukawa Matsuri
古川まつり

This festival is famous for its *taiko* (drum) performance known as *okoshi-daiko..*
● Apr. 19 - 20 ● Keta Wakamiya-jinja Shrine: Furukawa-shi, Gifu

Izumo-taisha Daisairei
出雲大社大祭礼

This is the biggest festival in the San'in district (in the north-west part of Honshū). It features a variety of very formal ceremonies.
● May 14 - 16 ● Izumo-taisha Shrine: Taisha-machi, Shimané

Kané Kuyō
鐘供養

This is a re-enactment of an old legend in which a princess turns into a snake and burns a priest to death.
● Apr. 27 ● Dōjō-ji Temple: Kawabé-chō, Wakayama

Funabutai
船舞台

A "floating festival", with plays and *hayashi** performances on boats floating on a creek.
● May 3 - 5 ● Okihata-suitengū Shrine: Yanagawa-shi, Fukuoka

Aofushigaki Shinji
青柴垣神事

In this ceremony based on a mythical tale, two married couples put to sea in two boats. The boats have leafy branches *(aofushi)* at each of their four corners and are enclosed in canopies.
● Apr. 7 ● Miho-jinja Shrine: Mihonoseki-machi, Shimané

Tanigumi Odori
谷汲踊り

The performers of this dance carry on their backs decorated *shinai* (bamboo swords) made from split bamboo 4.3 m. long, and beat drums while dancing.
● Feb. 18, Apr. 3, Aug. 15
● Kegon-ji Temple: Tanigumi-mura, Gifu

71

山王まつり
Sannō Matsuri

● Jun. 10 - 16 ● Hié-jinja Shrine: Chiyoda-ku, Tōkyō

The main *Sanno Matsuri* is held every two years, alternating with the *Kanda Matsuri* (see p. 54). In the Edo Era*, this festival was known as *Tenka Matsuri* and was attended by the *shōgun**. One of its best-known events is the *Ōchō*-style* *Shinkō** *Gyōretsu* parade held on Jun. 15.

Shinkō Gyōretsu
In this parade, two Imperial carriages with about 400 followers dressed in costumes of the Heian Era* (9th - 12th century) make their way through Akasaka, Yotsuya, Ginza, and Shimbashi.

Hōō
This legendary Chinese bird, similar to the phoenix, is thought to bring good luck.

Hōren
(Imperial carriage) No. 1

In the Edo Era, over 40 festival floats could be seen at the *Sannō Matsuri*, but now, only 3 *mikoshi* appear.

Miko Kagura
The *miko* (shrine maidens) of Hie-jinja perform *kagura* * dedicated to the gods.

Hōren
(Imperial carriage)
No. 2

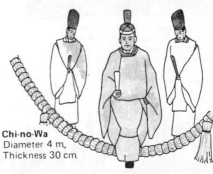

Chi-no-Wa
Diameter 4 m,
Thickness 30 cm.

Gubusha
(Imperial attendants)

Chi-no-Wa Shinji
In this ceremony, a year's good luck is said to be assured by passing, twice to the left and once to the right, through a large hoop made of bunches of *chigaya* (a kind of grass) tied round a bamboo frame.

チャグチャグ馬子
Chagu-Chagu Umako

● Jun. 15 ● Takizawa-mura, Morioka-shi, Iwaté

This festival, held in celebration of the god of horses, is unique to horse-breeding districts. About 100 beautifully-accoutered horses file in procession from Komagata-jinja Shrine to Morioka Hachimangū Shrine, a distance of 15 km, as a prayer for the safety of horses and the prosperity of their owners.

Nejiri-hachimaki
headband

Child rider

"Chagu-chagu" refers to the sound of the bells that the horses wear around their necks, while *"umako"* is a dialect word for *uma*, horse. The riders in the procession are usually children and young women.

The sight of the horses and riders winding their way along the paths between the rice paddies in summer, after the planting, is pure poetry. A dance called *Nambu-yossharé* is performed during the procession.

相馬野馬追い
Sōma Nomaoi

● Jul. 23 - 25 ● Sōma-shi, Fukushima

This festival, which was started in the 10th century, was originally a form of training for *bushi* (warriors). The best-known parts of the festival are *Katchū-keiba* (medieval-style horse races) on Jul. 23 and *Shinki-sōdatsusen* (a mock battle for holy flags) on Jul. 24. Both of these are magnificent spectacles which re-enact how Japanese warriors of olden times dressed and fought.

The *mikoshi** of *Ōta-jinja* Shrine. The shrine deity observes the battle from the *mikoshi*.

A *samurai** general about to take the field.

Shinki-Sōdatsusen
A red, a yellow and a blue flag *(Shinki)* are shot high into the air from a cannon, and the riders strive to gain possession of them as they reach the ground. This event starts at noon at Hibarigahara.

The ritual music and dancing performed at shrine and temple festivals in Japan includes *dengaku, nō*, kyōgen*, and kabuki**. These performing arts are designed to please the gods and secure their favor. They are most often seen at New Year festivals invoking blessings for the coming year, spring rice-planting festivals, and autumn harvest festivals.

Kurosawa Dengaku

黒沢田楽

Originally a rice-planting ritual (see p.34), *dengaku* is a form of music and dancing which has become an art in its own right. Since the 12th century it has become more and more influenced by *nō* and has come to be known as *dengaku-nō*. *Kurosawa Dengaku* is famous for preserving the original form of *dengaku*.

● Jan. 6 ● Hōfuku-ji Temple: Hōrai-chō, Aichi

Takigi-nō

薪能

Performed at Kōfuku-ji Temple (see p.15), this is the oldest of all the forms of *nō*.

● May 11 - 12 ● Kōfuku-ji Temple: Nara-shi, Nara

Mibu Kyōgen

壬生狂言

In this version of *kyōgen*, performed at Mibu-dera Temple, the actors perform various mimes while chanting prayers to Buddha. The *Tsuchigumo* dance is particularly well-known, and the whole performance is famous for its incorporation of the elements of both *nō* and *kyōgen*.

● Apr. 21 - 29 ● Mibu-dera Temple: Kyōto-shi, Kyōto

Taiko-nori Kabuki

太鼓乗り歌舞伎

Kabuki is performed on top of a 1 m. diameter *ōdaiko* (big drum).

● Jan. 14 ● Fujiki Dōsojin: Enzan-shi, Yamanashi

Hinoemata Kabuki

檜枝岐歌舞伎

This form of *kabuki* has been handed down from the Edo Era* (17th — 19th century), when it was performed in farming communities. While *dengaku* and *nō* were considered serious rites, *kabuki* was the farmers' entertainment.

● May 12 ● Atago-jinja Shrine: Hinoemata-mura, Fukushima

JUL. 7 祇園まつり
Gion Matsuri

● Jul. 1 - 29 ● Yasaka-jinja Shrine: Kyōto-shi, Kyōto

The *Gion Matsuri*, one of Japan's most important festivals, was begun in the 9th century by the *machishū* (inhabitants) of Kyōto. It lasts for one month, and the biggest events are *Yoiyama* (the eve of the festival) on Jul. 16 and *Yamahoko-junkō* on Jul. 17.

Kanko-hoko

Aburatenjin-yama

油天神山

- Get off at Kyōto Station on the Tōkaidō Shinkansen Line.
- *Yamahoko-junkō* starts at 9:00 a.m. on Jul. 17 proceeding along three streets, Shijōdōri, Kawaramachidōri and Oikedōri. Both sides of Oikedōri-Street are lined with viewing seats (for which a fee is charged).
- *Shinji* (shrine festivals) are held at Yasaka-jinja Shrine on Jul. 10 and 15.

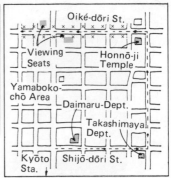

Yamabushi-yama

Kakkyo-yama

Kikusui-hoko

Yamahoko-junkō

Yama are mountain-sized festival floats which weigh 1.2 - 1.6 tons and are drawn by teams of 10 to 20 people. The roofs carry a cedar tree with dolls and other decorations. There are 24 of these floats in current use. *Hoko* are even bigger floats, 20 m. high, weighing 10 tons, and with wheels 2 m. in diameter. 7 of these, together with the 24 *Yama*, make up the huge parade that is *Yamahoko-junkō*.

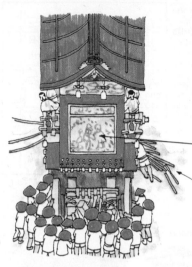

The central part of a *hoko* features a display of dolls *(Niwatori-hoko)*.

Miokuri — A tapestry featuring the history of Rome. *(Kanko-hoko).*

Tsuji-mawashi — To enable the *hoko* to turn more easily when going round corners, bamboo sprinkled with water is laid under the wheels.

Funa-hoko

Uradé-yama

Shinkōsai

On the evening of Jul. 17, 4 *mikoshi* are taken out of Yasaka-jinja Shrine. One of these, shown here, is the heaviest *mikoshi* in Japan.

Byōbu Matsuri

In this custom, which takes place at *Yoiyama,* people open the doors of their houses to show off their antique *byōbu* (folding screens) to the people watching the festival.

Sagi-mai

This dance to the spirit of herons takes place at Yasaka-jinja Shrine on Jul. 17.

Kikusui-hoko

Aburatenjin-yama

Hakata Gion Yamagasa

● Jul. 1 - 15 ● Kushida-jinja Shrine: Fukuoka-shi, Fukuoka

Many festivals in other parts of Japan have come to be termed *"Gion Matsuri"* in emulation of the famous festival of that name at Kyōto; and the *Gion Yamagasa* festival at Fukuoka is the biggest of these. The exciting *"Oiyama"* race early in the morning of July 15 is an event not to be missed.

Yamagasa
Festival floats are called *Yamagasa* in Fukuoka. There are two types, the *kazariyama* type (fixed floats), and the *kakiyama* type used in the *Oiyama* race.

Kakiyama weigh about 1 ton and are carried by a team of 28. Followers swell this number to several hundred.

Oiyama
This event is a race in which teams dash with their *kakiyama* along a 5 km. course.

● Get off at Hakata Station on the Sanyō Shinkansen Line.
● The *Oiyama* race starts at 4:59 a.m. on July 15.
● *Kakiyama* appear from July 10. The festival builds up through the events called *Oiyama-narashi* on 12 and *Shūdan yama-misé* on 13 to its culmination on July 15 with *Oiyama*.

Costume worn for Gion Yamagasa

Shioitori
On Jul. 1, all those taking part in the festival gather sand from the seashore as a purification rite. The sand is placed in boxes and hung underneath the *yamagasa*.

Nejiri hachimaki
A headband made from a twisted towel

Happi
Short coat

Shimekomi
Traditional underwear

Ichiban yamagasa
Float No. 1

Niban yamagasa
Float No. 2

各地の祇園まつり
Other Gion Festivals

The *Gion* festival, started in Kyōto, was originally a rite to ward off sickness. Later, its gorgeously-decorated festival floats and unique *gion-bayashi* music became popular all over Japan.

Narita Gion-é
成田祇園会

10 floats and a large number of *mikoshi* are paraded through the streets in this festival.
● Jul. 7 - 9 ● Naritasan Shinshō-ji Temple: Narita-shi, Chiba

A friendly demon who frightens off the spirits of sickness.

Tajima Gion Matsuri
田島祇園まつり

This festival is known for its *kabuki-yatai*, floats on which *kabuki** is performed.
● Jul. 19 - 21 ● Tadeuga-jinja, Kumano-jinja Shrine: Tajima-machi, Fukushima

Yamaguchi Gion Matsuri
山口祇園まつり

This festival is famous for the graceful dance known as *Sagi-mai*, in which the dancers are costumed as *sagi* (snowy herons).
● Jul. 20 - 27 ● Yasaka-jinja Shrine: Yamaguchi-shi, Yamaguchi

Tobata Gion Ōyamagasa

戸畑祇園大山笠

The *Nobori-yamagasa* (festival floats with flags) paraded during the day become *Chōchin-yamagasa* (festival floats with lanterns) at night. 9 m. high, these *Chōchin-yamagasa* are enormous pyramids of light.

● Jul. 13 - 15 ● Hachiman-jinja Shrine: Kitakyūshū-shi, Fukuoka

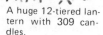

A huge 12-tiered lantern with 309 candles.

Kokura Gion Daiko

小倉祇園太鼓

The main attraction at this *Gion* festival is the *taiko* (drum) performances.

● Jul. 10 - 12 ● Yasaka-jinja Shrine: Kitakyūshū-shi, Fukuoka

Kan (the front face of the drum)

Doro (the rear face)

The *taiko* are about 50 cm. in diameter and are mounted on the front and back of the floats. Each of the 4 drummers takes one side of one of the drums.

管絃祭
Kangensai

● Jun. 17 by the lunar calendar* ● Itsukushima-jinja
Shrine: Miyajima-chō, Hiroshima

This ship festival has been famous since olden times. *Mikoshi* are placed before a large *torii* (shrine gate) called *Ō-torii* that stands in the sea, and *gagaku* is performed. Gaily-decorated ships sail past in procession. At night, lamps are lit on the ships, providing a beautiful spectacle.

Gagaku — A unique type of music that has been performed mainly for the Imperial Court and the nobility since the 10th century.

The *hōren*-*mikoshi** into which the holy spirit has descended, being carried across the water.

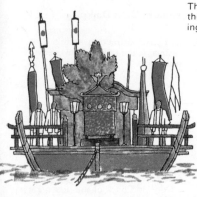

A *gozasen* consisting of three ships joined together side by side. This is used as a stage on which *gagaku* is performed, using *sangen* (three stringed instruments), *sankan* (three wind instruments) and *sanko* (three percussion instruments).

和霊大祭
Warei Taisai

● Jul. 23 - 24 ● Warei-jinja Shrine: Uwajima-shi, Ehime

This festival, started in the 18th century, is the most spectacular of Ehime Ken's summer festivals. Many spectators gather to see the hundreds of ships with their colorful *tairyōbata* flags in the harbor, the *Ushioni* that parades around the town, the *Hashiri-komi* ceremony, and other events unique to this festival.

Ushioni — A strange creature that looks like a cross between a whale and a dragon. It is about 7 m.long and is carried around the town by 15 to 20 young people.

In the *Hashiri-komi* ceremony, young people bear *mikoshi* energetically into the sea to the accompaniment of rockets. Others scramble for *sasataké*, thought to bring good fortune to the one who secures it.

天神まつり
Tenjin Matsuri

●Jul. 24 - 25 ● Ōsaka-tenmangū Shrine: Ōsaka-shi, Ōsaka

This is one of Japan's three biggest festivals. It is a lively festival with numerous events, such as the *Rikutogyo* (a parade of *mikoshi* through the city), the *Funatogyo* (a parade of ships), performances of special music called *danjiri-bayashi*, and firework displays.

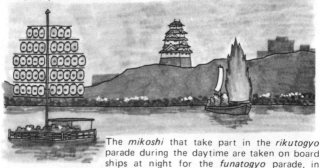

The atmosphere is heightened by the special music known as *Danjiri-bayashi,* performed on *Danjiri* (small festival floats) constructed in the precincts of Ōsaka Tenmangū Shrine. The sound of this music is described onomatopoetically in Japanese as *"kon-kon-chiki-chin"*.

The *mikoshi* that take part in the *rikutogyo* parade during the daytime are taken on board ships at night for the *funatogyo* parade, in which about eighty ships sail up the Dōjimagawa River.

浜降り祭
Hamaorisai

●Jul. 15 ● Samukawa-jinja Shrine: Samukawa-machi, Kanagawa

Hamaori is a type of festival in which *mikoshi* are carried over the sea. In some festivals, known as *Kaijōtogyo*, the *mikoshi* are taken on board ships, while in others, known as *kaichū-togyo*, the *mikoshi* are carried into the sea. *Hamaorisai* is one of the best known *Kaichūtogyo* festivals.

When the *misogi* (purification rite) in the sea is over, a ceremony is held on the shore.

In the early hours of the morning, 30 or more *mikoshi* are taken down to the shore. They are then carried with noisy cries and much jostling into the sea. The rowdier the festival, the happier the gods will be.

ねぶた/ねぷた
Nebuta/Neputa

The original purpose of this lively summer festival, held before harvesting was started, was to ward off sleepiness lest it interfered with the work. In a ceremony called *neburi-nagashi*, the spirits of sleep were cast into the river to be carried away to the sea. The name of this festival is pronounced *nebuta* or *neputa* depending on the district where it is held.

Aomori Nebuta

青森ねぶた

The main feature of this festival is the huge, wide *nebuta* figures striking *kabuki* poses. These figures are remarkable for their intensity of expression.

● Aug. 2 - 7 ● Aomori-shi, Aomori

The shape of the *nebuta* is formed by constructing a framework of bamboo and wire; this is then covered in paper, and the design is painted on the paper. Some *nebuta* are 10 m. high; the reason why they are broader than they are high is to avoid fouling power lines.

At the *Aomori Nebuta*, hundreds of dancers wearing flowered *hanagasa** hats join hands and dance to light-hearted *hayashi** music.

The *ōdaiko* (big drum) used at the *Aomori Nebuta* is about 3 m. in diameter, and is beaten by several drummers at once.

Hirosaki Neputa
弘前ねぷた

This festival is famous for its great fan-shaped *neputa* with their gorgeous designs derived from Chinese narrative scrolls, depicting brave warriors fighting. The *Hirosaki Neputa* festival is also called *Shingun Kenka Neputa*.

● Aug. 1 - 7 ● Hirosaki-shi, Aomori

The *hayashi** music played at the *Hirosaki Neputa* festival is of a more sombre and mournful tone than that of the *Aomori Nebuta* festival.

The front of the *neputa* depicts warriors fighting, while the back contrasts these scenes with charming pictures of beautiful women.

Kingyo Neputa
Children holding paper goldfish also parade at the festival.

Kuroishi Neputa
黒石ねぷた

More *neputa* are displayed at this *neputa* festival than at any other. The *neputa* are of various designs and include ones like those appearing at the Aomori and Hirosaki festivals.

● Aug. 1 - 7 ● Kuroishi-shi, Aomori

● From Tōkyō to Aomori takes 5.5 hours by Tōhoku Shinkansen and limited express, or 1 hour and 45 minutes by plane.
● From Aomori to Hirosaki takes 30 minutes by train.

> **Shachihoko** — A fabulous dolphine-like fish often used to decorate the topmost roofs of Japanese castles. It has large black scales and its tail is raised high above its head.

Noshiro-no-Nebunagashi
能代のねぶ流し

In this ceremony, also called *Shachi-nagashi*, castle-shaped lanterns topped with a bamboo basketwork *shachi* are lit and cast adrift on a river to carry away the spirits of sleep.

● Aug. 6 - 7 ● Noshiro-shi, Akita

七夕
Tanabata

The *Tanabata** festival is held in various parts of the country. On *Tanabata* night (Jul. 7 by the lunar calendar), many families display decorations made from *tanzaku** attached to bamboo poles. These simple decorations form the basis for the elaborate and colorful paper displays at the big *Tanabata* festivals of Sendai and Hiratsuka. *Tanabata* is now held on Jul. 7 by the modern calendar, but the big festivals are held on Aug. 7.

Sendai Tanabata Matsuri

仙台七夕まつり

Sendai's *Tanabata* festival is one of the three biggest, and millions of visitors flock to this city during the *Tanabata* season.

● Aug. 6 - 8 ● Sendai-shi, Miyagi

Tanabata Etôrô Matsuri
七夕絵灯ろうまつり

At this festival, huge paper lanterns painted with pictures of *ukiyoé**-style beauties or popular show-business personalities are displayed along the main streets.
● Aug. 6 - 7 ● Yuzawa-shi, Akita

Kaijô Tanabata Matsuri
海上七夕まつり

20 beautifully-decorated fishing boats, many bearing 20 m. bamboo poles with up to 30,000 red *tanzaku* attached, assemble and cruise around Bay.
● Aug. 7 - 8 ● Rikuzentakata-shi, Iwaté

Kenka Tanabata
けんか七夕

The main attraction at this festival is a jostling match between festival floats decorated with tens of thousands of *tanzaku*.
● Aug. 7 - 8 ● Rikuzentakata-shi, Iwaté

Matsumoto-no-Tanabata
松本の七夕

Tanabata is celebrated in the Matsumoto district by displaying various *Tanabata* dolls made of paper, including some in the form of loving couples and some wearing children's *kimono*.*
● Aug. 7 ● Matsumoto-shi, Nagano

提灯まつり
Chōchin Matsuri

Chōchin* lend color to many festivals. At some festivals, large numbers of *chōchin* are used to create beautiful decorations and heighten the mood; chief among these are Akita's *Kantō* festival and Nihonmatsu's *Chōchin Matsuri*.

Stunts such as balancing the *kantō* on shoulder or chest are performed.

Kantō
竿灯

Kantō are large decorations made from a 10 m. bamboo pole with 9 cross-poles from which are hung 46 *chōchin*. Each *kantō* is said to weigh as much as 60 kg. The 160 *kantō* displayed at this festival are a fantastic sight.

● Aug. 5 - 7 ● Akita-shi, Akita

Shirakawa Chōchin Matsuri
白河提灯まつり

This festival gets its name from the large number of *chōchin* accompanying the *mikoshi* in their parade.
● Sep. 13 - 15 (every other year in even years) ● Kashima-jinja Shrine: Shirakawa-shi, Fukushima

Nihonmatsu Chōchin Matsuri
二本松提灯まつり

7 *taikodai* (festival floats decorated with *chōchin*** and carrying *taiko*) parade around the town playing *matsuribayashi* (festival music).
● Oct. 4 - 6 ● Nihonmatsu-jinja Shrine: Nihonmatsu-shi, Fukushima

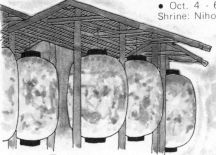

Isshiki-no-Ōchōchin Matsuri
一色の大提灯まつり

In this unusual festival, Suwa-jinja Shrine is decorated with 12 huge *chōchin* 10 m.high and 6 m.in diameter.
● Aug. 26 - 27 ● Suwa-jinja Shrine: Isshiki-chō, Aichi

大文字送り火
Daimonji Okuribi

● Aug. 16 ● Kyōto-shi, Kyōto

Okuribi is a fire lit to send the souls of deceased ancestors on their way after they have returned to this world for the *bon** festival. In the *Daimonji Okuribi* festival, 5 mountains *(gozan)* are used as the stage for an *okuribi* of huge proportions. The festival starts at 8:00 p.m., when fires are lit on Mt. Nyoigataké to form the Chinese character *dai*, meaning "large". After this, more fires are lit separately on each mountain to form different patterns.

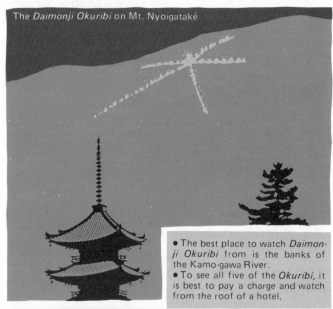

The *Daimonji Okuribi* on Mt. Nyoigataké

● The best place to watch *Daimonji Okuribi* from is the banks of the Kamo-gawa River.
● To see all five of the *Okuribi*, it is best to pay a charge and watch from the roof of a hotel.

Sectional View of Fire Grates

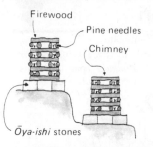

Firewood

Pine needles

Chimney

Ōya-ishi stones

Daimonji   *Jitō*

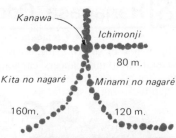

Kanawa

Ichimonji

80 m.

Kita no nagaré   *Minami no nagaré*

160m.   120 m.

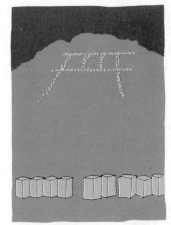

The "Toriigata" of Mt. Mandara-yama, and Arashiyama Mantō-nagashi

At the same time as the *okuribi* fires of *Daimonji Gozan* are being lit, paper lanterns are floated down the rivers. The *torii* represents a shrine.

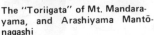

Mt. Matsugasaki, one of the *go-zan.* The west mountain features the character *myō,* meaning "mira-culous", while the east mountain features *hō,* meaning "doctrine". These *okuribi* are lit at 8:10 p.m.

The *"funagata" okuribi* on Mt. Myōkenzan, in the shape of a ship. (Lit at 8:15 p.m.)

99

AUG. 8 花笠踊り
Hanagasa Odori

● Aug. 6 - 8 ● Yamagata-shi, Yamagata

This is one of the four biggest festivals in the *Tōhoku* region. Several thousand dancers carrying *hanagasa* (painted paper hat) form ranks and dance through the city, cheered on by a happy throng of spectators.

Crying *"Yassho! Makasho!"*, the dancers dance along in unison to the rhythm set by the *hanagasa* songs.

As they dance, the dancers twirl their *hanagasa* left, right, up and down.

<table>
<tr><td>AUG.
8</td><td>阿波踊り
Awa Odori</td><td></td></tr>
</table>

● Aug. 12 - 15 ● Tokushima-shi, Tokushima

Awa Odori is a dance that is popular over the whole of Japan. At this festival, more than 200 groups dance around to the jaunty, light-hearted music. The spectacle of the nimble, high-spirited dancing of the men and the tilted *torioigasa* hats of the women is infectiously cheerful.

Men's dance

Awa Odori dance step

One of the best-known *awa-odori* choruses is "*Odoru ahō ni miru ahō. Onaji aho nara odora-nya son son!*", which means, roughly, "Since we dancers and you watchers are both crazy, you're crazy if you don't dance."

Women's dance

綱火
Tsunabi

Tsunabi are Japanese-style fireworks made by filling bamboo tubes about the size of a relay baton with gunpowder. These are then attached to long ropes and fired off so that they run along the rope. In olden times, they were used for communications or to set fire to high places, but now they are confined to use in festivals in various parts of Japan.

Katsuragiryū Tsunabi
葛城流綱火

There are 60 traditional performances combining *Tsunabi* puppets and *hayashi** music.

● Sep. 13 ● Hitokotonushi-jinja Shrine: Mitsukaidō-shi, Ibaraki

Karakasa Mantō
からかさ万灯

Originally a ritual used in praying for rain, this festival features large *kasa* (bamboo hats) 4 m. in diameter and 4 m. high, which are set on fire by *Tsunabi* from a *torii** 100 m. away.

● Aug. 17 ● Washi-jinja Shrine: Niihari-mura, Ibaraki

Takaokaryū Tsunabi
高岡流綱火

At the Takaoka festival, *Tsunabi* are attached to puppets, which appear to be performing in space when they are shot along the ropes.

● Jul. 23 by the lunar calendar*
● Atago-jinja Shrine: Ina-mura, Ibaraki

雨乞い/虫送り
Amagoi / Mushiokuri

Amagoi is a ritual prayer for rain, while *Mushiokuri* is a rite to drive away harmful insects, usually involving the lighting of *taimatsu* (torches) or the ringing of bells. Both rituals are practiced in farming communities all over Japan.

Sobué-no-Mushiokuri
祖父江の虫送り
Dolls made of straw, called *shanemorisama,* are burned in this festival to keep harmful insects from the rice plants.
● Jul. 10 ● Sobué-chō, Aichi

Také-no-Nobori
岳の幟
The participants in this rain festival climb a local mountain before dawn and make *nobori* (banners). They descend the mountain with these banners and parade around the villages.
● Jul. 15 ● Bessho-jinja Shrine; Ueda-shi, Nagano

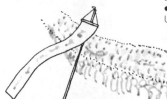

Suneori-no-Amagoi Gyōji
脚折の雨乞行事
In this rain rite, a 36 m. long and weighing 2 tons dragon, made from straw and bamboo leaves on a bamboo frame, is carried into a local lake.
● Aug. 8 (once every 4 or 5 years) ● Shirohigé-jinja Shrine: Tsurugashima-machi, Saitama

夏のまつり
Summer Festivals

Ishizaki Hōtōsai
石崎奉灯祭
This festival features six 15m. long, 2 m. wide floats called *kiriko*, fitted with giant lanterns.
● Jun. 15 by the lunar calendar *
● Hachiman-jinja Shrine: Nanao-shi, Ishikawa

Kawase Matsuri
川瀬まつり
Gaily-decorated festival floats called *kasa-hoko* are drawn around the town.
● Sep. 20 ● Chichibu-jinja Shrine: Chichibu-shi, Saitama

Fuji-no-Yamabiraki
富士の山開き
This festival is held to open the climbing season and pray for the safety of the two million or so people who visit Mt. Fuji each year.
● Jul. 1 ● Komitake-jinja Shrine: Fujiyoshida-shi, Yamanashi

Nagasaki Pēron
長崎ペーロン

This boat race festival, which uses special boats called *pēron,* has been carried on in Nagasaki for over 300 years. Recently, it has taken on more of the flavor of a sport.

● The first Sunday in Aug.
● Nagasaki-shi, Nagasaki

Nachi Himatsuri
那智火まつり

Teams bringing *mikoshi* down from the summit of the mountain and teams carrying *taimatsu* (torches) up from the foothills meet in the middle, where they engage in a tussle.

●Jul. 14 ● Kumanonachi-taisha Shrine: Nachikatsuura-chō, Wakayama

Hōju
— a large pointed ball representing fire.

Tamatori-Sai
玉取り祭

A fire tower is built in the sea off the main entrance to *Itsukushima-jinja* Shrine, and a "*hōju*" is hung from it. Good fortune is said to come to the youth who removes it from the tower and takes it to the shrine.

● The nearest Sunday to Jul. 18 by the lunar calendar*
● Isukushima-jinja Shrine: Miyajima-chō, Hiroshima

Festival Foods

まつりの食べ物

Another enjoyable aspect of festivals is the variety of special foods prepared and displayed. Many of these traditional foods were devised as a form of thanksgiving and as a prayer for good harvests in the coming year.

Ikinari Dango
(Kumamoto-ken)
A sweetmeat made from rounds of *satsuma-imo* (sweet potato) spread with *an* (sweet bean jam) and steamed.

Kawagoe-imo no sato-zuké
(Saitama-ken)
A sweetmeat made from steamed *satsuma-imo* preserved in sugar.

O-hassun
(Hiroshima-ken)
Shrimp, *gobō* (burdock root), *shiitake* (edible fungus), carrots and other ingredients are boiled and artfully arranged in a bowl measuring *hassun* (about 24 cm.) in diameter.

Mehari-zushi (Wakayama-ken)
Onigiri (rice balls) mixed with chopped cooked *katsuo* (bonito) and wrapped in *takana* (leaf mustard) leaves.

Matsuri-zushi
(Okayama-ken)
A form of *chirashi-zushi* consisting of fish and *sansai* (wild plants) on top of vinegared rice in a bowl.

Asuka-nabé (Nara-ken)
Chicken, *gobō* and other ingredients poached in milk.

Shiitaké-meshi (Miyazaki-ken)
Rice cooked with *Shiitaké.*

Itoko-ni
(Yamaguchi-ken)
A boiled dish of *zenzai* (thick sweet bean soup) with *tako* (octopus).

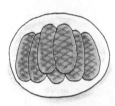

Shōyu-mochi
(Ehime-ken)
A simple sweetmeat made from rice, soy sauce and sugar.

Shikishi-mochi
(Ōita-ken)
A square *mochi** containing *an.*

Ninniku to tako no aemono
(Okinawa-ken)
A vinegared dish of *ninniku* (garlic) and *tako* (octopus) preserved in soy sauce.

Noppei-jiru
(Hiroshima-ken)
Chicken and other ingredients of *o-hassun* made into soup.

遠野まつり
Tōno Matsuri

●Sep. 14 - 15 ● Tōnogō-hachimangū Shrine: Tōno-shi, Iwate

This is an autumn festival held in supplication for a good harvest. Various traditional arts are performed, such as *Shishi-odori* (lion dance), *Taué-odori* (rice-planting dance), *Kagura* (sacred music and dance) and *Yabusamé* (horseback archery). The festival is well-known for its unique style of festival music, called *Nambu-bayashi*.

Wearing voluminous cloth capes, the Tōno dancers perform the lighthearted Aozasa-shishi-odori dance to the rhythm of the *taiko*.

Kagura is performed in the humorous *okamé* * and *hyottoko* *masks.

Beautifully-costumed children in the *Chigo-gyōretsu* (children's parade).

Women perform *nambu-bayashi* in the grounds of the shrine.

鶴岡八幡宮例大祭
Tsurugaoka-hachimangū Reitaisai

● Sep. 14 - 16 ● Tsurugaoka-hachimangū Shrine: Kamakura-shi, Kanagawa

The eve-of-festival ceremonies are held on the 14th, there is a parade of 3 *mikoshi* on the 15th, and the traditional event known as *Yabusamé*, said to have been continued since the 12th century, is held on the 16th. The *Yabusamé* ceremony features 3 archers dressed in the Kamakura Era*(12th century) hunting costume known as *karishōzoku*, riding their horses at high speed and shooting arrows at targets.

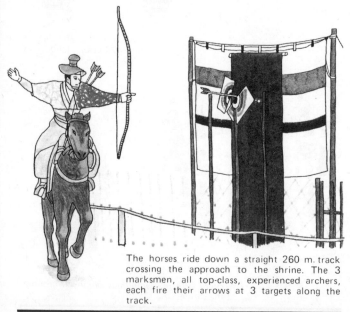

The horses ride down a straight 260 m. track crossing the approach to the shrine. The 3 marksmen, all top-class, experienced archers, each fire their arrows at 3 targets along the track.

SEP. 9
会津白虎まつり
Aizu Byakko Matsuri

● Sep. 22 - 24 ● Aizuwakamatsu-shi, Fukushima

This festival reconstructs the scene of an army taking the field for the battle known as *Boshin-no-Eki** (1868). It features a parade of 700 warriors, led by the elite *Byakkotai* corps.

Hakoné Daimyō Gyōretsu*
箱根大名行列

This parade depicts a parade of *daimyō* (feudal barons) crossing Mt. Hakoné in the Edo Era (17th - 19th century). It features 150 participants, all dressed in the costume of the times.
● Nov. 3 ● Hakoné-machi, Kanagawa

Jidai Matsuri

● Oct. 22 ● Heian-jingū Shrine: Kyōto-shi, Kyōto

This festival, sponsored by Heian-jingū Shrine, is said to include the most spectacular of the parades in Kyōto's autumn festivals. *Jidai Matsuri* literally means "Festival of the Ages", and the marchers in the parade are dressed in the costumes worn by nobles and ordinary people down through the ages during which Kyōto was the capital of Japan.

The parade starts with the 19th century and continues back to the 8th century, with a total of 1700 marchers in 20 groups taking part. The parade leaves Kyōto Gosho at noon and takes about two and a half hours to reach Heian-jingū.

The Kamakura Era*(1192 — 1333)
A *Yabusamé* (archers on horseback) parade, common among the *samurai*.

The Heian Era*(794 — 1192)
Onono Komachi, a poetess of the **Heian** Era, said to have been a matchless beauty.

The Edo Era*
(1603 — 1868)
A parade of women wearing *uchikaké,* a coat worn over *kimono* on ceremonial occasions.

The Azuchi-Momoyama Era*(1573 — 1603)
The warrior general Hashiba Hideyoshi in full armor.

The Meiji Era*
(1868 — 1912)
A parade recalling the *Ishin Kinnō-tai* (revolutionary army) of the start of the Meiji Era.

長崎くんち
Nagasaki Kunchi

●Oct. 7 - 9 ● Suwa-jinja Shrine: Nagasaki-shi, Nagasaki

Kunchi is a local dialect word from an area in the north of Kyūshū meaning "autumn festival". The Nagasaki Kunchi festival is a lively affair with a cosmopolitan atmosphere. Various festival dances such as the colorful *Ja-odori* are performed.

Kawabuné (Riverboat)

Ja-odori
(Snake dance)

After the dances, 3 *mikoshi* are carried at a fast pace down the steps.

The dancers dance their way around the city.

A graceful dance performed by *geisha**.

The Dutch-influenced *"Oranda Manzai**"

● The dances are held at Suwa-jinja Shrine, Kōkaidōmaé, Otabisho, Isegū and Yasaka-jinja Shrine.
● To see the festival at leisure, the best place is the seating provided by the Chamber of Commerce and Industry in front of the Kōkaidō. (5:00 p.m. on the 7th and 8:00 a.m. on the 8th).

上野天神まつり
Ueno Tenjin Matsuri

● Oct. 23 - 25　●Sugawara-jinja Shrine: Ueno-shi, Mié

The high point of this festival is the Oni-gyōretsu (parade of demons), said to have been started in the hope of halting a plague. Over 100 "demons" lead the parade on the Oct. 25, followed by *Shichifukujin*-odori* dancers, 9 festival floats, *mikoshi* and other attractions.

The *Oni-gyōretsu* proceeding around the town. The "demons" all wear different devil masks.

Chōshō-ki　　　　**Gyōdōmen-shitennō**　　　　**Hachitenki no Aka-oni**

Kawagoé Hikawa Matsuri

● Oct. 14 - 15 ● Hikawa-jinja Shrine: Kawagoé-shi, Saitama

In the *hon-matsuri* (full festival) held every other year, 17 richly-decorated parade floats are displayed along with numerous *mikoshi*. These floats are said to be replicas of those belonging to Tōkyō's Kanda-jinja Shrine.(see P.54)

It has become impossible to parade large floats around the center of Tōkyō because of the overhead power lines and telephone cables that festoon the city. For this reason, the *Kawagoé Hikawa Matsuri* is now the only occasion on which the huge, richly-decorated floats of old Edo can be seen taking part in festivals.

The highlight of the festival is the ceremony known as *Hikkawasé*, which takes place at evening. The floats gather together and crash into each other in the center of the town, and the *hayashi** bands compete noisily, trying to make the others lose their rhythm. The noise and excitement can rival those that of any other festival.

鹿踊り
Shishi Odori

The *Shishi Odori* (deer dance), performed by young boys, has been a tradition in Ehime Prefecture since the beginning of the 17th century. Boys representing male deer beat *kodaiko* (small drums) and dance lightly as they search for a female deer hiding from them. Together with *ushi-oni*, this dance is one of the highlights of the autumn festivals in this prefecture.

Uwatsuhiko-jinja Aki Matsuri

宇和津彦神社秋まつり

This festival is famous for its graceful dance known as *Yatsushishi-odori* (eight deers dance).
● Oct. 29 ● Uwatsuhiko-jinja Shrine: Uwajima-shi, Ehime

| Hōnai-chō | Misaki-chō | Uwajima-shi | Shirokawa-chō |

出雲大社神在祭
Izumo-taisha Jinzaisai

● Oct. 11 - 17 by the lunar calendar*● Izumo-taisha
Shrine: Taisha-machi, Shimané

In the month of October by the lunar calendar, all the gods
from all over Japan are supposed to gather at Izumo-taisha
Shrine. This month is known as *Kamiarizuki* (the month when
the gods are present) at Izumo, and *Kannazuki* (the month
when the gods are absent) in all other districts. At Izumo-taisha,
various solemn ceremonies are carried out for the benefit of
the assembled gods.

The gods are welcomed at the seashore and the procession then
makes its way towards Izumo-
taisha.

Kumano-taisha Kiribisai
熊野大社鑚火祭
In this festival, a *kiné* (a wooden
pestle for pounding rice) and an
usu (a wooden mortar), made that
year at Kumano-taisha Shrine, are
ceremonially handed over to
Izumo-taisha.
● Oct. 15 ● Kumano-taisha
Shrine: Yakumo-mura, Shimané

Hachinohé Sanja Taisai
八戸三社大祭

This festival is known for its parade of elaborately-constructed floats featuring scenes from folk tales and *kabuki*.

● Aug. 1 - 3 ● Ogami-jinja, Shinra-jinja, Jinmyōgū Shrines: Hachinohé-shi, Aomori

Shinjō Matsuri
新庄まつり

It takes the young people of each area a month to make the colorful floats, decorated with *kabuki* scenes, used in this festival. The floats are followed by *hayashi-renchū* (festival music bands) playing the local festival music called *Shinjō-bayashi* on flutes, drums, and other instruments.

● Aug. 24 - 26 ● Tozawa-jinja Shrine: Shinjō-shi, Yamagata

Morioka Hachimangū Matsuri
盛岡八幡宮まつり

The floats used in this festival, decorated with dolls representing famous heroes, are paraded to the stirring rhythm of *kodaiko* (small drums) played by boys leading the way and *ōdaiko* (large drums) played by youths bringing up the rear.

● Sep. 14 - 16 ● Morioka-hachimangū Shrine: Morioka-shi, Iwate

Hōrai Matsuri
ほうらいまつり

In this festival, a good harvest is prayed for by displaying 4 m.high dolls decorated with ears of rice, chestnuts, carrots, eggplants, cucumbers, red peppers, and other produce.

● Oct. 2 - 3 ● Kinkengū Shrine: Tsurugi-machi, Ishikawa

Daiyokkaichi Matsuri
大四日市まつり

The huge 6 m. high Ōnyūdō doll displayed at this festival represent a Buddhist priest, and is said to have been made originally to drive away evil spirits in the form of *tanuki** (raccoon dogs), thought to bewitch people.

●Aug. 1 - 4 ●Yokkaichi-shi,Mié

Ushimado Aki Matsuri
牛窓秋まつり

The highlight of this festival is the elaborate *mifune-danjiri*, festival floats in the form of ships.

● The fourth Sunday in Oct.
● Ushimado-jinja Shrine: Ushimado-chō, Okayama

Festival Toys and Crafts

まつりの玩具・民芸品

Chagu-chagu umako
(Iwaté-ken)
Wooden dolls in the shape of horses.

Ōgi Neputa
(Aomori-ken)
The *ōgi* (fan), with its sideways-spreading shape, represents prosperity.

Haneto Ningyō
(Aomori-ken)
The dancers at the *Aomori Nebuta* festival are called *haneto*.

Kantō Ningyō
(Akita-ken)
This is modelled on the *kantō,* a large triangular framework festooned with paper lanterns.

Bonden (Akita-ken)
The *Bonden Matsuri* doll.

Namahagé (Akita-ken)
A devil doll with a humorous expression. .

Kamakura (Akita-ken)
Inside the *kamakura* are dolls in the form of children.

Shishi-odori (Iwaté-ken)
Shishi-odori (deer dance) doll.

Ushioni (Ehimé-ken)
A cow-devil with a droll expression.

Sagi-mai (Shimané-ken)
A simple doll made of bamboo.

Koshidaka-tora (Fukushima-ken)
A papier mâché tiger.

Gion-hoko (Kyōto-fu)
A miniature of the *hoko* (festival floats) displayed at *Gion Matsuri*.

Nagoya-no-dashi (Aichi-ken)
A miniature of the float that used to appear at festivals in Nagoya.

Rōsharei (Mié-ken)
A bell in the shape of a festival float.

123

唐津くんち
Karatsu Kunchi

● Nov. 2 - 4 ● Karatsu-jinja Shrine: Karatsu-shi, Saga

The highlight of this festival is the 14 elaborately-constructed *yama* (festival floats) that are paraded around the town. All of the floats are over a century old, starting with 1st float (named *Akajishi*), built in 1819, through to the 14th float built in 1876; and they all present a magnificent spectacle.

8th float
Kinjishi (the golden lion) 1847

9th float
Takeda Shingen no Kabuto (the helmet of Takeda Shingen) 1864

11th float
Shutendōji to Minamoto no Yorimitsu no Kabuto (the robber Shutendōji and the helmet of Minamoto no Yorimitsu*). 1869

On the second day the floats are taken to Nishi no Hama Shore, where they are pulled across the dunes. Great strength is needed to pull them, since they sink into the sand, and even the spectators can be seen tensing their muscles in sympathy.

1st float
Akajishi (The red lion)
1819

2nd float
Aojishi (The blue lion)
1824

3rd float
Urashima Tarō* to Kamé (Urashima Tarō and the turtle) 1841

4th float
Minamoto no Yoshitsuné no Kabuto (The helmet of Minamoto-no-Yoshitsuné) 1844

5th float
Tai (The sea bream)
1845

6th float
Hōō-maru (The phoenix) 1846

7th float
Hiryū (The flying dragon) 1846

10th float
Uesugi Kenshin no Kabuto (The helmet of Uesugi Kenshin*) 1869

13th float
Shachi (The fabulous dolphin) 1876

125

Zuiki Matsuri
ずいきまつり

This festival is noted for its *okashi-mori, mikoshi* about 95 cm. high and 120 cm. wide, each constructed of about 400 *zuiki* (the stems of the *sato-imo,* or taro), together with persimmons, chestnuts and artificial flowers.
● Oct. 14 ● Mikami-jinja Shrine: Yasu-chō, Shiga

Aki Matsuri
秋まつり

This festival features a procession of gorgeously-decorated *futon-yatai,* festival floats with gaily-colored cushions on their roofs.
● Oct. 13 - 14 ● Soné-tenmangū Shrine: Takasago-shi, Hyōgo

Mega-no-Kenka Matsuri
妻鹿のけんかまつり

Three *mikoshi* proceed through the streets of the city, crashing energetically into each other.
● Oct. 14 - 15 ● Matsubara-hachimangū Shrine: Himeji-shi, Hyōgo

Kameyama-hachiman Aki Matsuri
亀山八幡秋まつり

In this festival, *mikoshi* with five layers of large *zabuton* (cushions) are whirled and shaken around.
●Oct. 16 ● Kameyama-hachimangū Shrine: Ikeda-chō, Kagawa

Saijō Matsuri
西条まつり

A spectacular festival featuring five *taikodai* and more than 40 *danjiri* (festival floats).
● Oct. 15 - 16 ● Isono-jinja, Ishioka-jinja Shrine: Saijō-shi, Ehimé

Sōhei Matsuri
僧兵まつり

This festival recalls the *sōhei* (fighting monks) of the 9th – 15th centuries. A variety of ceremonies take place, such as *sōhei-daiko* (drumming) and *sōhei-mochitsuki* (rice pounding); and an unusual burning *mikoshi*, called *sōhei-kaen-mikoshi,* is paraded after dark.
● Oct. 8 - 10 ● Sangaku-ji Temple: Komono-chō, Mié

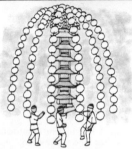

Honmon-ji-no-Oeshiki
本門寺のお会式
This festival is worth seeing for the beautiful *Mantō-gyōretsu* (lantern parade) held at night.
● Oct. 11 - 13 ● Honmon-ji Temple: Ōta-ku, Tōkyō

Myōkensai
妙見祭
The unusual feature of this festival is a *kida,* a cross between a turtle and a snake, consisting of a 2 m long snake's head on a 6 m long turtle's body.
● Nov. 17 - 18 ● Yatsushiro-jinja Shrine: Yatsushiro-shi, Kumamoto

Wakehime-jinja Reisai
和気比売神社例祭
A dance called *Funa-odori* is performed on a stage consisting of three ships joined together.
● Oct. 6 - 7 ● Wakehime-jinja Shrine: Matsuyama-shi, Ehimé

Hitoyoshi Kunchi
人吉くんち
This festival is noted for its unusual *Oniki - no - usudaiko-odori* dance.
● Oct. 9 - 11 ● Aoiaso-jinja Shrine: Hitoyoshi-shi, Kumamoto

Kansui-no-Kakiodori
寒水のかき踊り
In this dance, *shinai* (bamboo swords) with artificial flowers in 5 colors are worn on the dancer's backs and waved up and down, left and right.
● Sep. 8 - 9 ● Hakusan-jinja Shrine: Myōgata-mura, Gifu

Yagorōdon Matsuri
弥五郎どんまつり
At this festival, a 6 m. tall doll called *Yagorōdon* makes its appearance.
● Nov. 3 - 5 ● Iwakawa-hachiman-gū Shrine: Ōsumi-chō, Kagoshima

Tsu-no-Aki Matsuri
津の秋まつり
The main attraction at this festival is the amusing *Tōjin-odori* (Chinese dance).
● Oct. 10 ● Hachiman-jinja Shrine: Tsu-shi, Mié

秩父夜まつり
Chichibu Yomatsuri

● Dec. 2 - 3 ● Chichibu-jinja Shrine: Chichibu-shi, Saitama

Many spectators gather to watch the gorgeously-decorated festival floats being pulled through the streets at this festival. The festival is particularly lively and spectacular after nightfall — hence the name *Yomatsuri, which means 'night festival'.*

Kabuki* and *Hiki-odori* dancers are performed on the floats during the daylight hours.

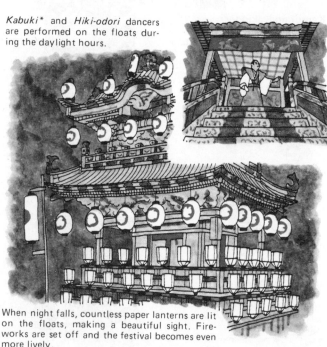

When night falls, countless paper lanterns are lit on the floats, making a beautiful sight. Fireworks are set off and the festival becomes even more lively.

奥三河の花まつり
Okumikawa-no-Hanamatsuri

● Kitashidara-gun, Aichi

This festival stretches over the period from the end of November to the beginning of January, with various *Hana-odori* (flower dances) and other events being held. The *Hana-no-mai* and *Oni-no-mai* dances performed by young boys add to the simplicity and mysteriousness of this festival.

Ohiruchara — featuring the *kagura* figures *okamé** and *hyottoko**.

Sakaki-oni
The demon of the flower festival, called *Sakaki-oni*, appears brandishing a *sakaki,* or sacred *Shintō** branch.

Young boys perform the *hana-no-mai* dance around a *yugama* (cauldron).

* This festival is held from the last part of Nov. to the first part of Jan.

● Dec. 31 ● Oga-shi, Akita

In this festival, men representing gods in the guise of demons enter people's houses to warn the children against laziness. The festival is also thought to guarantee a good harvest and ensure the safety of the houses and their occupants. The *namahagé*'s costume consists of a straw *mino* (cape) covering his whole body, and a mask with a fearsome expression. This festival is celebrated mainly in the north of Japan.

The *namahagé* carry a *teoké* (wooden pail) and a wooden *deba-bōchō* (kitchen knife).

The *namahagé* is welcomed with food.

Amahagé
あまはげ

Young men wearing demon masks tour the town admonishing children against idleness.

● Jan. 1, 3, 6 ● Yuzamachi, Yamagata

Uchiura-no-Amamehagi
内浦のあまめはぎ

Young boys dressed as demons visit the houses.

● Feb. 3 ● Uchiuramachi, Ishikawa

Minatsuki-no-Amamehagi
皆月のあまめはぎ

● Jan. 6 ● Monzenmachi, Ishikawa

The *Namahagé* is also known as *Amahagé* or *Amamehagi*, depending on the locality.

Toshidon
トシドン

In this old custom, men with devil masks known as *Toshidon* warn children against bad behavior and give them rice cakes called *toshidon-mochi*. Although this custom is observed in the south of Japan, it resembles the *Namahagé* festivals of the north.

● Dec. 31 ● Shimokoshi-mura, Kagoshima

Okurita-no-Amamehagi
大栗田のあまめはぎ

● Jan. 15 ● Murakami-shi, Niigata

133

アイヌのまつり
Ainu Festivals

The *Ainu* is an indigenous people of Hokkaidō and adjacent islands with their own unique customs and culture. Most *Ainu* festivals are solemn rites based on their particular religious faith.

An *Ainu* woman playing the *kuchi-biwa,* a lute play-ed with the mouth.

Kushiro Kotan Matsuri
釧路コタンまつり

A *kotan* is an *Ainu* community, and a *Kotan Matsuri* is a festival of thanksgiving to the deity who watches over a particular community. The *Kushiro Kotan Matsuri,* a festival dedicated to the god of lakes, is quiet and restrained.

● The 2nd Sunday in Sep. ● Kushiro, Hokkaidō

Orochon-no-Himatsuri
オロチョンの火まつり

This is the fire festival of the people who live on the shores of the Sea of Okhotsk. Wearing unique costume, the participants dance round a fire, intoning solemn words of prayer.
● The 4th Saturday and Sunday in Jul. ● Abashiri, Hokkaidō

The head of a bear god offered at the altar during the *Iomanté*

Shiraoi-no-Iomanté
白老のイオマンテ

The *Iomanté* festival, also known as *Kuma Matsuri* (bear festival), is the most solemn of the hunting *Ainu's* festivals, and originally involved the sacrifice of a baby bear captured and raised for this purpose. The bear was thought to be returned to heaven by this practice. The sacrifice is not actually carried out nowadays.
● The 1st Saturday and Sunday in Feb. ● Shiraoi-chō, Hokkaidō

The festival of the Okinawa district, the islands in the extreme south of Japan formerly known as the *Ryūkyū* Kingdom, are unique both in their content and in their relation to the seasons. Many of them are highly unusual.

Naha Tsunahiki
那覇綱引き
In this tug-of-war, which lasts for hours, several thousand people pull and strain at a rope 1 m. in diameter and 100 m. long.
● Oct. 8 - 10 ● Naha-shi, Okinawa

Yonabaru Tsunahiki
与那原綱引き
● The nearest Sunday to Jun. 15 by the lunar calendar*
● Yonabaru-chō, Okinawa

A *mezuna* ('female rope') and an *ozuna* ('male rope') are coupled together. This is said to represent the sex act.

Minatogawa Hārī
港川ハーリー
In this boat race, the village is divided into east and west teams, and small boats called *sabani* are raced by crews numberng 14 to 15.
- May 14 by the lunar calendar*
- Gushikami-son, Okinawa

Bon Bozé
盆ボゼ
This dance is used at the end of *bon-odori** to drive away evil spirits. It is interesting for its strange bamboo basketwork masks.
- Jul. 16 by the lunar calendar*
- Toshima-mura, Kagoshima

Hassaku Odori
八朔踊り
The highlight of this dance is the energetic and vociferous *men-odori*.
- Aug. 1 by the lunar calendar*
- Mishima-mura, Kagoshima

Izaihō
イザイホー
All the island's women who have reached the age of 30 are initiated as *miko* (shrine maidens, called *nanchu* in the local dialect) in this solemn ceremony.
- Nov. 15 - 18 by the lunar calendar (once every 12 years)*
- Chinen-son, Okinawa

Tokyo Fairs
東京の市

The word *ichi* (fair, or market) is said to have been derived from the word for festival, and it is certainly true that many fairs are held in the grounds of shrines or temples. The stalls at these fairs are simply constructed and usually sell good-luck charms and talismans which people think will bring a good harvest or will help them to get on in the world.

Ōji-Inari-no-Tako-Ichi (Kite Fair)
王子稲荷の凧市

The kites sold at this fair are said to help prevent fires, since kites cut through the wind (and, by analogy, reduce the wind's power to fan flames).
● Hatsu-uma* in Feb. ● Ōji-Inari-jinja Shrine: Kita-ku, Tōkyō

One of the *daruma* doll's eyes is painted in when a wish is made, and the other eye is painted in if the wish comes true.

Jindai-ji-no-Daruma-Ichi (Daruma Doll Fair)
深大寺のダルマ市
● Mar. 3 - 4 ● Jindai-ji Temple: Chōfu-shi, Tōkyō

Ofujisan-no-Ueki-Ichi (Garden Fair)
お富士さんの植木市
● May 31, Jun. 1 Jun. 30, Jul. 1
● Sengen-jinja Shrine: Taitō-ku, Tōkyō

Hōzuki-Ichi
(Lantern Plant Fair)
ほおずき市
This fair started with the selling of *hōzuki* (lantern plants) to eliminate harmful insects. It is believed that visiting the shrine on July 10 will afford the same number of blessings as having visited the shrine on 46,000 other days.
● Jul. 9 - 10 ● Sensō-ji Temple: Taitō-ku, Tōkyō

Asagao-Ichi
(Morning Glory Fair)
朝顔市
This fair is said to have started as a competition among professional gardeners to see who could grow the best morning glory.
● Jul. 6 - 8 ● Kishibojin, Taitō-ku, Tōkyō

Peel off the outer skin, pinch the 'lantern' to soften the contents, and remove the seeds through a small hole. A noise can be made by blowing on the empty 'lantern'.

Nihombashi-no-Setomono-Ichi
(Pottery Fair)
日本橋のせともの市
● The middle of Jul. ● Hamachō Park: Chūō-ku, Tōkyō

Ninomiya-no-Shoga-Ichi (Ginger Fair)
二宮の生姜市

Shōga (ginger) is said to prevent stomach upsets.

● Sep. 9 ● Ninomiya-jinja Shrine: Akikawa-shi, Tōkyō

Bettara-Ichi
べったら市

Bettara is a type of pickle made from *daikon* (Japanese radishes).

● Oct. 19 - 20 ● Takarada Ebisu-jinja Shrine: Chūō-ku, Tōkyō

Tori-no-Ichi
酉の市

Lucky rakes supposed to bring good fortune are sold at this fair.

● Tori-no-hi*, in Nov. ● Ōtori-jinja Shrine: Taitō-ku, Tōkyō

Hagoita-Ichi (battledore fair)
羽子板市

A *Hagoita* is a wooden paddle used as a battledore in the traditional badminton-like game called *hané-tsuki*. The ones sold at the fair carry various decorations.

● Dec. 17 - 19 ● Sensō-ji Temple: Taitō-ku, Tōkyō

CURIOUS FESTIVALS

*

In many parts of Japan, ancient beliefs have produced some strange and interesting customs and festivals. These depict the richly-imaginative world of gods and demons, heaven and hell, that the Japanese of olden times created.

どろかけまつり
Mud-Slinging Festivals

Many festivals in Japan require the participants to strip down to their loincloths, wrestle, and cover each other in mud or charcoal. These festivals are both a prayer for a good harvest and a way of purifying oneself.

Dairokuten-no-Hadaka Matsuri
第六天の裸まつり
Youths wearing only a *fundoshi** make the trip from the shrine to the lake below and return covered with mud to purify themselves and pray for a good harvest.
● Feb. 25 ● Musubi-jinja Shrine: Yotsukaidō-shi, Chiba

Doronko Matsuri
どろんこまつり
Young people who have married since the previous year's festival cover themselves with mud and carry *mikoshi*.
● Apr. 3 ● Katori-jinja Shrine: Noda-shi, Chiba

Suminuri Matsuri
スミ塗りまつり
In this festival, ashes from New Year's decorations burnt at the *Sai-no-Kami* festival are mixed with snow, and the participants apply this mixture to each other's faces as a form of supplication for a trouble-free year.
● Jan. 15 ● Matsunoyama-machi, Niigata

強飯式
Gōhan Shiki

The ceremony known as *Gōhan* involves forcing people to eat rice, potatoes, *udon** and other food from huge dishes and to drink *saké* from large bowls. This type of festival is common all over Japan.

Rinnō-ji Gōhan Shiki
輪王寺強飯式
The *gōhansō* (priests of the *Gōhan* ceremony), dressed in *yamabushi** style, force the participants to drink *saké* from large bowls and eat mounds of white rice.
● Apr. 2 ● Rinnō-ji Temple: Nikkō-shi, Tochigi

Kodomo Gōhan Shiki
子供強飯式
In this humorous festival, children dressed as *yamabushi* force adults to eat large quantities of rice.
● Nov. 25 ● Ubuoka-jinja Shrine: Nikkō-shi, Tochigi

Hakkōji-no-Gōriki
発光路の強力
This *gōhan* festival is interesting for the amusing style in which the "feeders" force their victims to eat.
● Jan. 3 ● Myōken-jinja Shrine: Awano-machi, Tochigi

生殖に関するまつり
Festivals for Fertility

Some festivals in Japan celebrate the male and female sex organs or simulate sex. These festivals are held to pray for both plentiful progeny and bountiful harvests. Most of them are humorous and light-hearted.

Tagata-jinja Hōnen Matsuri
田県神社豊年まつり
In this festival, large wooden phalluses are carried about on *mikoshi*, in prayer for procreation and the sanctity of life.
● Mar. 15 ● Tagata-jinja Shrine: Komaki-shi, Aichi

Tsuburosashi
つぶろさし
In supplication for a good harvest, a male god holding a wooden phallus and a female god playing a musical instrument called a *sasara* perform *kagura* *.
● Jun. 15 ● Sugawara-jinja Shrine: Hamochi-machi, Niigata

Onda Matsuri
御田まつり
After the rice-planting ceremony, the participants perform a play representing a married couple having sex.
● The first Sunday in Feb.
● Asukaniimasu-jinja Shrine: Asuka-mura, Nara

144

恐山大祭
Osorezan Taisai

● Jul. 20 - 24 ● Entsū-ji Temple: Mutsu-shi, Aomori

The weathered surface of Mt. Osoré, located on the Shimokita Peninsula in the north of Honshū, looks like a vision of hell in its bleakness and grimness. This has led to the belief that the mountain is a gathering-place for dead souls. At the *Osorezan Taisai* festival, women known as *itako* call up these spirits, and tens of thousands of people visit the mountain to hear the voices of their dead relatives.

People waiting for the spirits to manifest themselves.

The *itako*, many of whom are blind, chant spells to conjure up the dead spirits.

A procession of priests crosses Mt. Osoré.

修行僧のまつり
Festivals by Priests under Training

Many of Japan's festivals include ceremonies carried out by priests undergoing training at temples or shrines. Through such mystical ceremonies, they express the depth of their faith and pray for the safety of all people.

Madara Kishinsai
マダラ鬼神祭

The holy fire known as *goma* is lit, and a strange *Oni-odori* (devil dance) is performed to the rhythm of *oni-daiko* (devil drums).

● The first Sunday in Apr.
● Amehiki Kannon Rakuhō-ji Temple : Yamoto-mura, Ibaraki

Goma — the name of a type of cedar burnt on Buddhist altars to drive away worries and evils.

Shirohebi-jinja-no-Hiwatari
白蛇神社の火渡り

In the ceremony known as *Hiwatari* (crossing the fire), monks walk barefoot on glowing charcoal to pray for people's good health.

● May 3 ● Shirohebi-jinja Shrine: Ueda-shi, Nagano

Ki-no-Jōjutsu
木の杖術

In this ceremony, the monks perform forms of the ancient martial art known as *jōjutsu*, using 1 m. staves of evergreen oak.

● Oct. 15 or the previous Sunday
● Ki-hachimangū Shrine: Tsuga-machi,

ひょうげまつり
Hyōge Matsuri

Hyōge means to joke and play the fool. In many Japanese festivals and folk arts, the participants dress in amusing costumes and perform droll activities.

Hyōge Matsuri
ひょうげまつり

In this festival, men wearing humorous masks and make-up carry *mikoshi* made of farm produce.

● The first Sunday in Aug. by the lunar calendar* ● Kagawa-chō, Kagawa

Chayamachi Oni Matsuri
茶屋町鬼まつり

A "devils' parade" of people wearing devil masks.

● The third Saturday and Sunday in Oct. ● Konpiragū Shrine: Kurashiki-shi, Okayama

Achi-jinja Aki Matsuri
阿智神社秋まつり

Men called *suinkyo* wearing amusing masks lead the way as *mikoshi* are paraded around the town.

● The third Saturday and Sunday in Oct. ● Achi-jinja Shrine: Kurashiki-shi, Okayama

147

鞍馬の火まつり
Kurama-no-Himatsuri

● Oct. 22 ● Yuki-jinja Shrine: Kyōto-shi, Kyōto

Kurama-no-Himatsuri (The Kurama Fire Festival) originated in the custom of lighting fires called *mukaebi* to guide gods or spirits from the other world on their visits to this world. All the local inhabitants turn out carrying *mikoshi* and torches big and small, and events reach their climax between 10:00 and 11:00 p.m. This mysterious festival is one of Japan's most important fire festivals.

The *taimatsu* (torches) are made from grass cut in June and left to dry until October.

Bathed in the light of torches, the *mikoshi* are carried on their way.

Children also take part in the festival, carrying torches.

白川村どぶろくまつり
Shirakawa-mura Doburoku Matsuri

● Oct. 10 - 19 ● Shirakawa-hachimangū, Hachiman-jinja
Shrine: Shirakawa-mura, Gifu

In this unusual festival, everyone drinks *doburoku** (unrefined local *saké)* to celebrate the autumn harvest. Many gaily-colored *nobori* (banners) are displayed, eight-legged lions perform *shishi-mai* (the lion dance), and *mikoshi* are paraded. At dusk, the villagers stage *niwaka-kyōgen** and other performances in the grounds of the shrines.

An eight-legged *shishi* (Chinese lion) leads a parade of *hayashi** bands and people carrying *nobori* (banners).

Children performing on the shō, a metal percussion instrument.

The home-made *doburoku* is passed around among the local inhabitants and visiting spectators alike.

動物に関するまつり
Festivals about Animals

Festivals which feature animals of one kind or another can be seen in various parts of Japan. In some of these, the animal is thought to be transformed into a god, and some are memorial services for animals that have been killed. Many of these festivals are humorous and light-hearted, and many feature dragons and other imaginary beasts.

Kinryū-no-Mai
金龍の舞
Weaving left and right, the *ryū* (dragon) used in this festival, meaning "dance of the golden dragon" is 14.5 m. long and weighs 75 kg.
● Mar. 18 ● Sensō-ji Temple: Taitō-ku, Tōkyō

Tsukuba-san Gama Matsuri
筑波山ガマまつり
This festival is held as a memorial service for all the *gama* (toads) killed in making toad grease.
● Aug. 1 - 2 ● Tsukubayama-jinja-Shrine: Tsukuba-machi, Ibaraki

Jagamaita
ジャガマイタ
Children parade with snakes made of bamboo, straw, rope, grass, and other materials.
● May 5 ● Oyama-shi, Tochigi

Uraga-no-Toraodori
浦賀の虎踊り
This unusual festival features a tiger instead of the usual *shishi* (Chinese lion) in the *Shishi-mai* (lion dance).
● The 2nd Saturday in Jun.
● Tametomo-jinja Shrine: Yokosuka-shi, Kanagawa

Kaeru Tobi
蛙とび
This festival tells the tale of a young man who was turned into a frog for maligning a *yamabushi*.
● Jul. 7 ● Zaōdō Temple: Yoshino-chō, Nara

Toyohama-no-Ōtai Matsuri
豊浜の大鯛まつり
At this festival, held to give thanks for good hauls of fish, huge *tai* (sea bream) 20 m. long are carried.
●The middle of Jul.
● Minamichita-chō, Aichi

Kingyo Matsuri
金魚まつり
This is a festival in celebration of *kingyo* (goldfish), said to have been dearly loved by Matsudaira Sadanobu, a vice-*shōgun* in the Edo Era.
● May 12 - 13 ● Chinkoku-jinja Shrine: Kuwana-shi, Mié

鬼
Demons

Japanese *oni* (demons) are usually fearsome-looking creatures with horns and fangs. They represent all manner of evils, and every part of Japan has festivals designed to exorcise them. Some demons are benevolent, however, and fight the devil as representatives of god.

Kiraigō
鬼来迎

This ceremony is a play set in the Buddhist hell, and features frightening masks representing red and black devils.

● Jul. 16 ● Kōsai-ji Temple: Hikari-machi, Chiba

Kodomo Ondeko
子供鬼太鼓

One of the most famous of Sado's traditional performing arts is *Ondeko,* in which the performers play *taiko* drums wearing devil masks.

● Apr. 1 - 30 ● Sadogashima, Niigata

Nafuné Taisai
名舟大祭

This festival is known for its *Gojinjo-daiko* drum music, played by drummers wearing a variety of weird masks.

● Jul. 31 - Aug. 1 ● Hakusan-jinja Shrine: Wajima-shi, Ishikawa

舞踏
Dances

The original purpose of the dancing that takes place in so many of Japan's festivals was to drive away evil spirits. It was thought that the spirits would be caught up in the dancing and driven far away by the noise of gongs and drums. Each locality has its own particular style of dance and costume.

Tokushigé Ubara-daiko Odori
徳重大バラ太鼓踊り

In this dance, the dancers wear *shiro-juban* (white under-garments) and *shiro-hachimaki* (white headbands), and carry drums on their chests.
● Sep. 14 by the lunar calendar*
●Tokushige-jinja Shrine: Ijūin-chō, Kagoshima

Meta Furyū
米多浮立

Furyū is a lively art in which drums and gongs are beaten by costumed performers. *Meta furyū* features a dance called *Tentsuki-mai* in which the dancers wear large half-moon-shaped decorations on their heads.
● The nearest Sunday to Oct. 20
● Ōimatsu-jinja Shrine; Kamiminemura, Saga

Suhōtei
数方庭

This dance features huge *nobori* (banners), 10 m. long and weighing about 60 kg.
● Aug. 7 - 13 ● Iminomiya-jinja Shrine: Shimonoseki-shi, Yamaguchi

仮面
Masks

Many festivals use masks representing people, animals, gods and demons. These are said to embody the way in which the Japanese think about divine spirits, and many masks are regarded as sacred and are carefully preserved.

Menkaké Gyōretsu
面掛行列

The participants in this parade display 10 different masks said to have been made in 1768.
● Sep. 18 ●Mitama-jinja Shrine: Kamakura-shi, Kanagawa

Oshiroi Matsuri
おしろいまつり

To pray for a good rice crop in the following year, flour made from the current year's rice is mixed with water and applied to the participant's faces in this festival.
● Dec. 2 ● Ōyamazumi-jinja Shrine: Haki-machi, Fukuoka

Mōja Okuri
亡者送り

In this festival, two priests wearing devil masks beat the ground inside the precincts of the shrine with torches and run from the shrine compound.
● Jan. 18 ● Sensō-ji Temple Taitō-ku, Tōkyō

The devil mask used in *Tenjin Matsuri*
天神まつりの鬼面

The devil mask used in *Ushi-matsuri*
牛まつりの鬼

The *Sakaki-oni* mask used in *Hanamatsuri*
花まつりの榊鬼

The devil mask used in *Amenomiya Shinji*
雨宮神事の鬼面

The *Bugaku* * mask used in *Amamiya-jinja*
天宮神社の舞楽面

The *shishi* (Chinese lion) mask used in the Sasara-odori dance.
ささら踊りの獅子

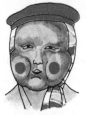
Tsuburosashi
つぶろさし

The *Yama-no-Kami* mask used in *Yama-bushikagura*
山伏神楽の山の神

その他の奇祭
Other Curious Festivals

Niramekko Obisha
にらめっこおびしゃ
In this festival, the contestants drink *saké* while staring each other in the eye. The first to laugh is the loser.
● Jan. 20 ●Komagata-jinja Shrine: Ichikawa-shi, Chiba

Nakizumō
泣き相撲
Sumō* wrestlers wearing *mawashi (sumō* belts) hold babies in their arms and rock them. The winner is the one whose baby cries first.
● Sep. 19 or the 4th Sunday in Sep. ● Ikiko-jinja Shrine: Kanuma shi, Tochigi

Yoshida-no-Himatsuri
吉田の火まつり
At this festival to mark the closing of the climbing season on Mt. Fuji, a large number of *taimatsu* (pine torches) 3 m. high and 1 m. in diameter are lit all at once. This is one of the three biggest "strange festivals" in Japan.
● Aug. 26 - 27 ● Fujisengen-jinja Shrine: Fujiyoshida-shi, Yamanashi

Oyama Matsuri
お山まつり
In this festival, the large boulders on the face of the mountain are celebrated as gods.
● Mar. 1 - 2 ● Noto-machi, Ishikawa

Idori Matsuri
いどりまつり
In this humorous festival, the participants make fun of such things as the dark color and small size of the *mochi**put out by the *dōmoto* (sponsor) of the festival.
● Nov. 7 ● Sugawara-jinja Shrine Noto-machi, Ishikawa

Ōyada-no-Hinkoko Matsuri
大矢田のヒンココまつり
This festival features myth-based puppet plays using primitive puppets.
● Apr. 15 ● Ōyada-jinja Shrine: Mino-shi, Gifu

Nakiri-no-Warajinagashi
波切のわらじ流し
3 m. long *waraji* (straw sandals) are floated out to sea in prayer for good hauls of fish.
● Saru-no-hi* in Nov. ● Nakiri-jinja Shrine: Daiō-chō, Mié

Inoko
亥の子
In supplication for a good harvest, children carrying *inokozuchi* (cudgels made of straw) tour the town beating the gardens of the houses.
● I-no-hi* in Oct. by the lunar calendar* ● Nosé-shi, Ōsaka

Takengei
竹ん芸
Young men wearing fox masks perform juggling tricks on top of double bamboo poles 15 m. high.
● Oct. 14 - 15 ● Wakamiya Inari jinja Shrine: Nagasaki-shi, Nagasaki

Warai Matsuri
笑いまつり
In this unusual festival, 12 *warai-otoko* (laughing men) all laugh together.
● Oct. 10 ● Niu-jinja Shrine Kawabé-chō, Wakayama

Bon Tsunahiki
盆綱引き
Children with soot all over their bodies have a tug-of-war with a 30 cm. thick rope.
● Aug. 15 ● Kumano-jinja Shrine: Chikugo-shi, Fukuoka

ANNUAL EVENTS

All of Japan's annual events have their roots far back in history. This section describes the ancient customs still celebrated in people's homes, and the festivals associated with these.

〔Annual Events〕
年中行事一覧

- Jan. 1st *(Shōgatsu)*
  New Year's Day
- Jan. 15 *(Seijin-no-hi)*
  Coming-of-Age-Day
- Feb. 3 *(Setsubun)*
  Bean-Throwing Ceremony
- Feb. 11 *(Kenkoku-kinembi)*
  National Founding Day
- Mar. 3 *(Momo-no-Sekku)*
  Hina-matsuri or Girl's Festival
- Mar. 21 *(Shumbun-no-hi)*
  Vernal Equinox Day

- Apr. 8 *(Hana-matsuri)*
  Buddha's Birthday Festival
- Apr. 29 *(Tennō-tanjōbi)*
  The Emperor's Birthday
- May 3 *(Kenpō-kinenbi)*
  Constitution Memorial Day
- May 5 *(Tango-no-Sekku)*
  Kodomo-no-hi or Children's Day
- Jul. 7 *(Tanabata)*
  The Star Festival
- Aug. 15 *(Bon)*
- Mid September *(Tsukimi)*
  Moon Viewing
- Sep. 15 *(Keirō-no-hi)*
  Respect-for-the-Aged-Day
- Sep. 23 *(Shūbun-no-hi)*
  Autumnal Equinox Day

- Oct. 10 *(Taiiku-no-hi)*
  Health-Sports Day
- Nov. 3 *(Bunka-no-hi)*
  Culture Day

- Nov. 15 *(Shichi-go-san)*
  Festival day for children of 3,
  5 and 7 years of age.
- Nov. 23 *(Kinrō-kansha-no-hi)*
  Labour Thanksgiving Day
- Dec. 31 *(Ō-misoka)*
  New Year's Eve

● = National holiday

大晦日／正月
Ōmisoka／Shōgatsu

The 31st of December *(Ōmisoka)* and the 1st of January *(Shōgatsu)* are very important in Japan, and various events and ceremonies are held on these days to mark the end of the old year and the beginning of the new. The aim of most of these ceremonies is to expurgate all the bad fortune of the past year and pray for good fortune in the coming year, and most people take the ceremonies very seriously. Along with *Bon**, *Shōgatsu* is Japan's most important festival.

Shishi-mai (see P.52)

Joya-no-kané

The ceremony known as *joya-no-kané* is held at temples all over Japan on *Ōmisoka*. The temple bell is rung 108 times, once for each of the 108 sins that man is heir to. The sins are thus driven out, and the new year can be started with a clean slate.

Hatsumōdé

This is the custom of going to shrine or temple in the period from midnight on New Year's Eve to the 7th of January to pray for health and happiness in the coming year.

At shrines in the Kyōto area, the elegant and refined pastimes of the old nobility are practiced at New Year.

Kemari
蹴鞠

Kemari, a game resembling soccer, became an amusement of the aristocracy in Japan in the 10th century. A ball made of deerskin is kicked into the air and must not be allowed to touch the ground. This traditional sport is still played at New Year in some areas.

● Jan. 4 ● Shimogamo-jinja Shrine: Kyōto-shi, Kyōto

Karuta-hajimé
かるた始め

This ceremony features the traditional card game known as *hyakunin-isshu.**The players are dressed in the elegant and beautiful costumes of the nobility of olden times.

● Jan. 3 ●Yasaka-jinja Shrine: Kyōto-shi, Kyōto

Karuta-tori

In this traditional card game, each card bears the second half of one of a hundred famous *tanka* (poems). The referee starts to read the first half of a poem, and the players grab the matching card as soon as they recognize it. The winner is the one who has the most cards at the end of the game.

Mōtsūji Matarajinsai
毛越寺摩多羅神祭
This ceremony is famous for the ancient dance known as Ennen-no-mai, performed by priests and children.
● Jan. 20 ● Mōtsū-ji Temple: Hiraizumi-chō, Iwate

Omato-shinji
お的神事
In this ceremony, usually held at the beginning of the year, children shoot arrows to drive away evil spirits.
● Jan. 15 ● Hachiman-jinja Shrine: Ichiba-chō, Tokushima

Shichifukujin-mai
七福神舞い
This humorous New Year's dance, featuring the *shichifukujin** is held to pray for good harvests in the coming year.
● Jan. 14 - 15 ● Nihonmatsu-shi, Shirosawa-mura, etc. Fukushima

節分
Setsubun

Setsubun is the period around Feb. 3 when winter turns into spring. The best known ceremony of *Setsubun* is the custom known as *Oni-yarai*, practiced in homes and shrines, in which soybeans are scattered around to drive out demons and bring in good fortune.

Setsubun-é
節分会
In this ceremony, a hundred *toshi-otoko** scatter *fuku-mamé* (lucky beans) and *fuku-mochi* (lucky rice-cakes). Many people gather to collect the beans and rice-cakes and thus receive good fortune.
● Feb. 3 ●Taga-taisha Shrine: Taga-chō, Shiga

Setsubun-é
節分会

This ceremony features a man wearing a golden mask with four eyes, driving away demons.
● Feb. 3 ● Heian-jingu Shrine: Kyōto-shi, Kyōto

Onioi-shiki
鬼追い式

The god *Bishamon-ten* drives away six devils in this ceremony.
●Feb. 3 ● Kōfuku-ji Temple: Nara-shi, Nara

Kihōraku
鬼法楽

Men in red, blue and black devil costumes dance on a stage and are then driven away in this *Setsubun* ceremony.
●Feb. 3 ● Rōzan-ji Temple: Kyōto-shi, Kyōto

Setsubun Oni-odori
節分鬼踊り

Devils of various colors take part in this amusing dance.
● Feb. 3 ● Honjō-ji Temple: Sanjō-shi, Niigata

桃の節句
Momo-no-Sekku

Momo no Sekku (*Hinamatsuri* or The Doll's Festival) is a festival for girls and is held on March 3. Families set up a display of *hina-ningyō* dolls in their homes, with *shiro-zaké* (white *saké* made from *saké* and rice malt), *hishi-mochi* (lozenge-shaped rice cakes) and peach blossoms; and many shrines hold special ceremonies for the occasion.

Nagashi-bina
流し雛

Several thousand *hina* dolls given as offerings to the shrine in the past year are placed in boats and sent out to sea.

● Mar. 3 ●Awashima-jinja Shrine: Wakayama-shi, Wakayama

Myōenji Hinamatsuri
妙円寺雛まつり

In this unusual festival, children are dressed as *hina ningyō* and arranged on a tiered platform like the dolls.

● The last Saturday in Feb. or the first Saturday in Mar. ● Myōen-ji Temple: Shibuya-ku, Tōkyō

端午の節句
Tango-no-Sekku

While *hinamatsuri* is for girls, *Tango no Sekku* (Children' Day)
is for boys. Families with boys display *koinobori* outside their
houses and *gogatsu-ningyō* (dolls dressed in *samurai**costume)
inside, in prayer that their children will grow up strong and
healthy.

Fukinagashi — pennants

Magoi — black carp,
for the father

Higoi — red carp,
for the mother

Koinobori
These banners in the shape of large,
colorful carp are made of cloth or
paper.

Gogatsu-ningyō
These dolls in the form of *musha
(samurai)* warriors) represent the
hope that the boys for whom they
are displayed will grow into
strong, fearless men.

Také-uma Matsuri
竹馬まつり
In this children's festival, children
march in procession astride bamboo horses, wearing *jingasa* (sol-
dier's hats).
●May 5 ● Wakamiya-hachiman-gū
Shrine: Shin-asahi-chō, Shiga

花まつり／練供養
Hanamatsuri／Nerikuyō

Hanamatsuri (Flower Festivals) are customarily held to commemorate the birthday of Buddha, on April 8. His statue is anointed with *amacha* (hydrangea tea) in celebration of the occasion.

Nerikuyō are festivals held to celebrete *raigō*, the coming of the *nijūgo bosatsu* (25 Buddhas) to this world. A parade of believers wearing Buddha masks depicts the Buddhas descending from Heaven and gives a glimpse of the sublime world of Buddhism.

Mambe onerikuyō
万部お練り供養
Jūbosatsu (10 Buddhas) parade with various musical instruments.
●May. 1 - 5 ● Dainenbutsu-ji
Temple: Ōsaka-shi, Ōsaka

Hanamatsuri

Hotoké-mai
仏舞
An elegant dance in which the dancers wear Buddha masks.

● May 8 ●Matsuodera Temple: Maizuru-shi, Kyōto

Nijūgo-bosatsu Raigō-e
二十五菩薩来迎会
Believers in the Buddhist faith cross a bridge wearing Buddha masks. This festival is known familiarly as *Kuhonbutsu no menkaburi*.

● Aug. 16 (once every three years)
● Jōshin-ji Temple: Setagaya-ku, Tōkyō

Nerikuyō Éshiki
練供養会式
This festival is famous for its re-enactment of the legend in which a princess is led to *gokuraku* (the Buddhist heaven). The actors in the ceremony wear special costumes and Buddha masks.

●May 14 ●Taima-dera Temple: Taima-chō, Nara

盆／精霊流し
Bon／Shōrō Nagashi

The word *bon* or *urabon* is the Japanese translation of the Sanskrit word Ullambana, the original meaning of which was "terrible affliction". In Japan, July 15 by the lunar calendar*is considered to be the day on which the souls of one's ancestors

Paper Tōrō   **Stone Tōrō**

The *tōrō* (lanterns) which carry the dead souls down the rivers to the sea are made by people for their own ancestors. Most of these lanterns are of paper and have lighted candles inside.

Miyazu-no-tōrō nagashi
宮津の灯籠流し
In this majestic ceremony, fireworks are set off and more than 10,000 lanterns are sent down the river.
● Aug. 16 ● Miyazu-shi, Kyōto

return to this world for a visit, and many families still observe the old ceremonies on or around this day. Typical rites include *haka-mairi* (visiting the graves of one's ancestors), *bon-odori (bon* dancing), the lighting of fires called *mukaebi* to welcome the dead souls and *okuribi* to send them on their way, and the custom of *shōrō-nagashi*, in which the spirits are sent down the rivers to the sea in paper boats. The most famous *okuribi* is the *Daimonji-okuribi* (see P.98)

Mito-no-Oshōro-nagashi
三戸のお精霊流し
The boats used in this ceremony are beautifully-decorated, 5m.long constructions made of straw on a bamboo framework. They are pulled into the sea by young boys and floated on their way.
● Aug. 16 ●Miura-shi, Kanagawa

Chūgoku bon-é
中国盆会
Chinese residents from all over Japan gather in Nagasaki for this *Bon* festival.
● Jul. 26 - 28 by the lunar calendar*
● Sōfuku-ji Temple: Nagasaki-shi, Nagasaki

Shārasen-nagashi
精霊船流し
In this ceremony, the souls of the deceased are sent down to the sea in decorated straw boats.
● Aug. 16 ● Nishino shima-chō, Shimané

盆踊り
Bon-Odori

Large numbers of people take part in the folk dancing that goes on all over Japan during the *bon** season. The custom is thought to have started as a way of welcoming and sending off the souls of people's ancestors on their periodic visits to this world. *Yagura* stages are assembled in town and village squares or in the grounds of shrines, and everybody dances in a circle round the *yagura* to the sound of *hayashi** music.

The *yagura* are festooned with lanterns and *taiko* drums, and other instruments are placed on them.

Nishimonai Bon-odori 西馬内盆踊り

The dancers at this festival cover their faces with black cloths to represent the dead.
● Aug. 16 - 18 ● Ugo-machi, Akita

Kanko-Odori カンコ踊り

A drum hung from the drummer's neck and suspended in front is called a *kanko*.
● Aug. 16 ● Chōsen-ji: Temple: Isé-shi, Mié

Ōmi-no-hōkaodori 大海の放下踊り

Here, the dancers wear large *uchiwa* (fans) on their backs and beat drums carried on their chests.
● Aug. 14 - 15 ● Shin-shiro-shi, Aichi

Jugoya sorayoi 十五夜ソラヨイ

This dance features child dancers wearing *mino**, *hakama**, and hats known as *yoi-yoi-gasa*.
● Aug. 15 by the lunar calendar* ● Chiran-cho, Kagoshima

Shanshan Matsuri しゃんしゃんまつり

The dancing in this festival is interesting for the colorful *kasa* (umbrellas) carried by the dancers.
● Aug. 16 ● Tottori-shi, Tottori

Yamaga Tōrō Matsuri 山鹿灯籠まつり

In this festival, women dance with *tōrō* (lanterns) on their heads.
● Aug. 15 - 16 ● Ōmi-ya-jinja Shrine: Yama-ga-shi, Kumamoto

花火大会
Hanabi Taikai

Since the technique for making fireworks was introduced into Japan in the 16th century, *Hanabi taikai* (Firework displays) have been held regularly in all parts of the country, especially during summer festivals. The most spectacular fireworks are the rockets known as *warimono*, developed in Japan, which explode in great starbursts representing chrysanthemums, wisteria, plum blossoms, cherry blossoms, and other flowers.

Waridama

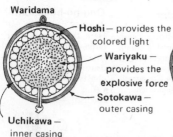

Hoshi — provides the colored light

Wariyaku — provides the explosive force

Sotokawa — outer casing

Uchikawa — inner casing

Tsuridama

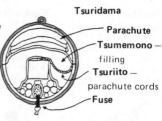

Parachute

Tsumemono — filling

Tsuriito — parachute cords

Fuse

Rockets are classified into two types, *waridama* and *tsuridama*. *Waridama* explode radially, their color changing 2 or 3 times, while *tsuridama* are suspended from parachutes and hive out their light as they drift down.

Sumidagawa Hanabi Taikai
隅田川花火大会
This famous firework display has a history of 250 years. It was discontinued in 1961 but revived in 1978 after a lapse of 17 years.
● The last Sunday in Jul.
● Sumida-gawa River, Tōkyō

月見／七五三
Tsukimi／Shichi-go-san

The full moon in September is considered to be the most beautiful of the year and is called *Chūshū no meigetsu* (harvest moon). Many families make arrangements of *susuki* (pampas grass), prepare *tsukimi-dango* (rice-flour dumplings), and view the moon at this time, and moon-viewing parties are held in some areas. The custom of viewing the moon is known as *tsukimi*.

Kangetsu-é
観月会

Since olden times, Ōsawa pond has been famous as a place for viewing the moon. On the night of the full moon in September and the night before, people go out on the pond to view the moon in boats with dragon's heads attached-ed.

● Full moon in mid-Sep.
● Daikaku-ji Temple: Kyōto-shi, Kyōto

Shichi-go-san
七五三

Along with *Momo-no-Sekku* (Mar. 3) and *Tango-no-Sekku* (May 5), and *Shichi-go-san*, held on Nov. 15, is a festival at which people pray that their children will grow up happy and healthy. Three-year-old girls, five-year-old boys, and seven-year-old girls are dressed in their best clothes (*haregi*, either colorful *kimono* or Western dress) and taken to shrines to pray.

OVERVIEW

1. Festivals and Seasons

Since the Japanese are historically a nation of farmers, their festivals are closely related to farming, and especially to the planting and harvesting of rice. Rice is planted in June and harvested in October; and all over the country, festivals are held in spring to pray for a good crop and in autumn to give thanks for the harvest.

Summer is the season when the growing crops are most threatened by natural phenomena such as typhoons, drought and disease, and the only way the people of olden times knew of averting such disasters was to pray. This was the purpose of festivals held in summer. Winter was thought to be the holiest of the four seasons, and the many solemn festivals held in various parts of the country on and around New Year reflect this belief.

Japanese festivals are thus divided into two overall groups; those held in spring and autumn, and those held in winter and summer.

2. Festival Days

In former times, the lunar calendar was used in Japan, and there were 29 to 30 days in each month. The days of the new moon, the full moon, and the half-moons, i.e., the 1st; the 7th or 8th; the 15th; and the 22nd or 23rd of each month, were treated as holy days. These days were known as *haré-no-hi*, as distinct from the other days of the month, known as *ké-no-hi*. Festivals were almost always held on *haré-no-hi*.

3. The Lunar (Old) and Solar (New) Calendars

The lunar calendar was abandoned in favor of the solar calendar in Japan in 1872. Since there is a disparity of approximately one month between the two, and since many festival days are still calculated on the lunar calendar, it is often difficult to know exactly when a particular festival is going to take place. The dates of festivals are decided by one of the following three methods:

1. One calendar month is added to the lunar-calendar date. Thus a festival held on July 7 according to the lunar calendar will be held on August 7.
2. The festival is held on the same date. Thus a festival held on July 7 according to the lunar calendar will still be held on July 7.
3. The festival day is still calculated according to the lunar calendar. Thus a festival held on July 7 according to the lunar calendar will be movable, falling on or about August 7. Many local festivals still follow this method.

4. Yoi-matsuri (the eve of the festival) and Hon-matsuri (the main festival day)

Many festivals start in the evening of one day and continue until the evening of the following day. This is because, in former times, people regarded a day as lasting from sunset to sunset; and so the eve-of-festival and the festival day itself were actually different parts of the same day. Since festivals were in principle held only on *haré-no-hi*, they could not usually last for more than 24 hours.

5. The Structure of a Festival

The purpose of a festival is to invite deities down from heaven and to pray with them for good fortune, a good harvest, etc. Festivals therefore consist of the following three parts:

1) **Kami mukaé** — a ceremony to welcome the gods to earth, usually held in a shrine or other sacred place.

2) **Shinkō** — the main event of the festival, in which the participants parade around the local community together with the gods, who are carried in the palanquins called *mikoshi*.

3) **Kami-okuri** — a ceremony in which the gods are respectfully sent back to where they live, since simply to abandon them at the end of the festival would be to invite diaster.

6. Japanese Religious Beliefs

Shintō, Japan's indigenous religion, has its roots in a polytheistic belief system, similar to shamanism and animism, in which all natural phenomena, such as fields, mountains, fire and water, were thought to contain the spirit of a deity. These are the deities celebrated at festivals. Eventually, when the Emperor system became established as a political system, this polytheism developed into true *Shintō*, in which Amaterasu Ōmikami, the Sun God and legendary ancestor of all the Emperors, is worshipped as the supreme deity.

Azuchi-Momoyama Era 安土桃山時代
1573 – 1602. The era after the Sengoku (Warring States) Era when Japan once again became a united country. Known for its ornate arts and crafts.

Bon 盆
July 15 by the lunar calendar (on or about 15 August by the solar calendar). Thought to be the day on which the souls of people's ancestors return to this world. (See p. 170)

Bon odori 盆踊り
The dances performed at the *bon* festival, to comfort the souls of the dead. (See p. 172)

Boshin-no-eki 戊辰の役
1868. One of the biggest battles of the Meiji Revolution, fought between the Emperor's forces (*kangun*) and the *Shōgun's* forces *(bakugun)*.

Bugaku 舞楽
A form of music and dance introduced from China in the 8th century, popular among the nobility of the time.

Chinese calendar 十二支
Consists of 12 year cycles, with each year in the series named after a different creature (rat, ox, tiger, rabbit, dragon, snake, horse, sheep, monkey, cock, dog, wild boar – in Japanese, *ne, ushi, tora, u tatsu, mi, uma, hitsuji, saru, tori, inu,i*). These 12 signs are called *jūni-shi*. They are usually used in conjunction with ten calendar signs called *jikkan*, and the total zodiac system thus contructed, the calculation of which is extremely complex, is called *eto*. It is closely related to the 12 Western zodiac signs.

Chōchin 提灯
A cylindrical lantern made of paper on a framework of split bamboo.

Daimyō gyōretsu 大名行列
In order to suppress the possibility of unrest, Edo Era *shōgun* would compel the *daimyō* (local lords) from all over Japan to make periodic visits to the capital, Edo (the present-day Tōkyō).

Since the *daimyō* had to be accompanied by large numbers of retainers, these visits were enormously expensive, leaving them little money for plotting revolution.

Doburoku どぶろく

Unrefined *saké*; i.e., *saké* from which the lees *(saké kasu)* have not been filtered. It is milky-white in color, and like other forms of alcohol, its production and sale are usually prohibited without a special licence. An exception is made for the *doburoku* consumed at the *doburoku-matsuri*, since it is made specially by local people for the festival and is not put on sale.

Edo Era 江戸時代

1603 – 1867. An age of great political stability in which Japan was controlled by the *shōgun,* starting with Tokugawa Ieyasu.

Fundoshi ふんどし

Men's traditional underwear in the form of a long loincloth.

Geisha 芸者

A highly-skilled entertainer who sings, dances and plays music at traditional parties. *Geisha-asobi* (*geisha* parties) were among the highest class of entertainment in the Edo Era.

Hakama 袴

Men's formal wear, in the form of a divided skirt.

Hanagasa 花笠

A bamboo or rush hat decorated with flowers, often seen at festivals.

Hatsu-uma 初午

The first "horse day" in February, the seventh day on the Chinese calendar.

Hayashi 囃子

Traditional music played on the *fué* (flute), *taiko* (drum), *shamisen* (three-stringed lute) and other instruments. The *hayashi* music played at festivals is called *matsuri-bayashi* and features a variety of different melodies depending on the locality.

Heian Era 平安時代

794 – 1191. Kyōto was the capital of Japan during this era, the golden age of culture among the aristocracy.

Hōren 鳳輦
A *mikoshi* (portable shrine) with a *hōō* (Chinese phoenix) mounted on top.

Hyakunin-isshu 百人一首
A collection of a hundred poems, each by a different poet. Many different such anthologies have been compiled during Japan's history.

Hyottoko ひょっとこ
A droll-looking mask of a man with one very small and one normal-sized eye, and lips pursed for breathing fire. Written with the Chinese characters for *hi* (fire) and *otoko* (man).

I-no-hi 亥の日
The twelfth day on the Chinese calendar.

Iwato-biraki 岩戸開き
According to legend, the world became dark when the sun god, *Amaterasu Ōmokami,* hid himself in a cave. To lure him out, a beautiful female goddess was said to have danced in front of the cave.

Kabuki 歌舞伎
One of Japan's unique traditional performing arts. At first performed only by women, it is now performed only by men. Known for its gorgeous costumes and elaborate sets. (See p. 76)

Kadomatsu 門松
A decoration made from pine branches, placed in front of houses at New Year.

Kagura 神楽
Sacred dance and music performed in homage to the gods. Said to have originated in the dance performed at *Iwato biraki.* (See p. 20)

Kamakura Era 鎌倉時代
1192 – 1333. A government formed at one of the most strife-torn periods in Japan's history. The great *samurai* families controlled the country during this era.

Kari-shōzoku 狩装束
The dress worn by *samurai* when practising falconry.

Kimono 着物
Japan's traditional dress.

Kirin 麒麟
A mythical beast resembling a unicorn.

Kurofuné 黒船
The warship in which Perry arrived to break Japan's many years of self-imposed isolation is known as *Kurofuné*, or "black ship".

Kyōgen 狂言
Humorous skits usually performed in the intervals of a *nō* performance. This genre was founded in the Heian Era.

Lunar calendar 旧暦
A calendar based on the waxing and waning of the moon. This calendar was used in Japan until the middle of the 19th century. Dates on it lag about a month behind those on the solar calendar. (See Overview)

Manzai 漫才
Comic dialogue.

Meiji Era 明治時代
1868 – 1912. The era when power was restored from the *shōgun* to the emperor, and Japan started to become a modern nation.

Mikoshi 神輿
A kind of portable shrine into which a god descends at festivals. (See p. 58)

Minamoto-no-Yoshitsuné 源義経
1159 – 1189. A legendary hero who was a military genius but who was treacherously overthrown by his own brother, became a vagabond, and finally committed suicide.

Mino 蓑
A rainproof cape made of straw.

Mochi 餅
A pounded rice cake made from special glutinous rice, often made at festivals and annual events.

Nanakusa 七草
7 seasonal plants, representing spring *(haru no nanakusa)* or autumn *(aki no nanakusa)*.

Nō 能

A form of masked play unique to Japan, known for its highly stylized sets and acting.

Ōchō style 王朝様式

In the style of the court at Nara and Heian Era.

Otafuku おたふく

A mask of a woman with a flat nose and round face. Usually used together with the *hyottoko* mask.

Ryū 竜

A mythical dragon-like beast thought to live in lakes or seas, bringing rain when it flies. It has a body like a snake's, horns like a deer's, eyes like a demon's, and ears like a cow's.

Sa-otomé 早乙女

A young girl planting rice.

Saiō 斎王

An unmarried queen dedicated to a shrine.

Saké 酒

Rice wine.

Samurai 侍

A Japanese warrior, also known as *bushi*.

Saru no hi 申の日

The ninth day on the Chinese calendar.

Sengoku Era 戦国時代

1467 – 1572. The era in which Japan was divided into a number of warring states. The era produced many famous heroes until it came to an end when Japan was reunited under Toyotomi Hideyoshi.

Shichifukujin 七福神

The seven gods of good fortune.

Shimé kazari 注連飾

New Year's decorations attached to a *shimé-nawa.*

Shimé nawa 注連縄

A straw rope hung up to keep out trouble.

Shinkō 神幸

A parade of deities. *Mikoshi* (portable shrines) usually head the parade, followed by *yatai* (festival floats).

Shintō 神道
Japan's traditional religion, which deifies the Emperor. (See Overview)

Shishi mai 獅子舞い
A dance designed to drive off deer, wild boar and other animals which damage crops. (See p. 52)

Shōgun 将軍
The highest military rank in old Japan. Usually refers to the *shōgun* who controlled the government in the Edo Era, when Japan was a military state.

Sumō 相撲
A form of wrestling peculiar to Japan. Two *rikishi* (wrestlers) wearing special *mawashi* (loincloths) fight in a circular ring.

Taimatsu 松明
A torch made from pine branches and bamboo.

Takeda Shingen 武田信玄
Takeda Shingen was known as a resourceful general and brilliant administrator. He was lifelong rivals with Uesugi Kenshin, the ruler of the neighbouring state, and, like him, died a natural death before succeeding in his campaign to become ruler of Japan.

Tanuki 狸
A mischievous pot-bellied, creature formerly thought to be capable of changing its form to that of a person, sake flask, etc.

Tanzaku 短冊
A long, thin strip of paper for writing *tanka* poems on. (See p. 32)

Tokugawa Ieyasu 徳川家康
The first *shōgun* of the Edo Era. A brilliant tactician and astute politician.

Tori-no-hi 酉の日
The tenth day on the Chinese calendar.

Torii 鳥居
A *shintō* shrine gate.

Tōrō 灯籠
A square lantern made of stone, bamboo, wood, etc., with paper pasted over the openings.

Toshi-otoko 年男
Since the Chinese calendar is based on a 12 year cycle, the year in which a person was born comes round again every 12 years. Men born in a year with the same sign as the current year are called *toshi-otoko,* while women are called *toshi-onna.*

Tsukimi dango 月見団子
A kind of *dango* (rice-flour dumpling) eaten while viewing the moon at the *tsukimi* festival.

Udon うどん
Noodles made from wheat.

Uesugi Kenshin 上杉謙信
Uesugi Kenshin was a brave general with strong principles and a straightforward disposition who is said to have kept aloof from women all his life. He dreamed of uniting all Japan under his rule, but died of an illness while leading his army on Kyōto, the capital of the country at that time.

Ukiyoé 浮世絵
Woodblock prints with natural scenes or portraits of beautiful women. This form of art was very popular in the Edo Era.

Urashima Tarō 浦島太郎
A legendary figure said to have visited the Queen of the Sea's underwater palace on the back of a turtle.

Yamabushi 山伏
Priests who retreat to the mountains as part of their Buddhist training. They are said to acquire supernatural powers in this way.

Yatai 屋台
Richly-decorated festival floats, first used at Kyoto's Gion Matsuri, and later in various parts of the country. They usually form part of *shinkō* parades, and some feature performances of *kabuki* or puppet plays. *Yatai* are also called *yama* (mountain), *hiki-yama* (pulled mountain), *yamagasa* (mountain hat), and *dashi* (mountain vehicle), depending on the locality.

Year of the Monkey 申年
The ninth year on the Chinese calendar.

Year of the Tiger 寅年
The third year on the Chinese calendar.

●Festival Calendar

AUGUST

The following works were used as reference when compiling this book.
'Nihon-no-matsuri' by Kōdansha
'Nihon-no-matsuri' by Rippū Shobō
'Shiki–Nihon-no-matsuri' by Mainichi-shinbunsha
'Nihon-no-matsuri' by Yama-to-keikoku-sha
'Matsuri-to-seikatsu' by Komine-shoten
'Nihon minzoku geinou jiten' by Daiichihouki
'Kyōdo-no-matsuri' by Ie-no-hikari kyōkai
'Nihon-no-matsuri' by Sankei-shinbunsha
'Nihon-no-gyōji matsuri jiten' by Sanseidō
'Tōkyō–Waga machi' by Hoiku-sha

ILLUSTRATED

FESTIVALS OF JAPAN

英文 日本絵とき事典　4

初版 発行　昭和60年7月1日
改訂3版　昭和62年9月1日
　　　　　（Sep.1, 1987 3rd edition）
編 集 人　斉藤晃雄
発 行 人　木下幸雄
発 行 所　日本交通公社出版事業局
　　　　　〒101 東京都千代田区神田鍛冶町3-3
　　　　　大木ビル8階（☎03-257-8391）
　　　　　海外ガイドブック編集部
印 刷 所　交通印刷株式会社

●

編集制作　株式会社アーバン・トランスレーション
イラスト　松下正己
表紙デザイン　東　芳純
翻　　訳　John Howard Loftus

交通公社発行図書のご注文は
日本交通公社出版販売センター
〒101 東京都千代田区神田須田町1-12
山萬ビル8階（☎03-257-8337）
振替　東京7-99201　送料（実費共）225円

定価　880円

863375　　712060
ISBN4-533-00489-X C2026 ¥880E